Geo. A Mitchell,   HUM
Glasgow, Scotland $\frac{S}{30}$
        to   A 1014431
LScam Parish,
    July 11, 1930.

D1212238

THE KIRK IN SCOTLAND

THE PROCESSION OF THE MODERATORS

THE
KIRK
IN
SCOTLAND
1560-1929

BY JOHN BUCHAN AND
GEORGE ADAM SMITH

HODDER & STOUGHTON

HOUSTON PUBLIC LIBRARY

R0159044912
HUM

INDEXED IN Subject
need

Made and Printed in Great Britain for HODDER AND STOUGHTON LTD.
by T. AND A. CONSTABLE LTD., Printers, Edinburgh

PREFACE

THIS book has been prepared at the request
of the leaders of the Church of Scotland,
who desired to have in some popular form
a memorial of the great events of last year.
The first and third chapters have been
written by Mr. John Buchan, and the
second by Principal Sir George Adam
Smith. The illustrations have been selected
and the title-page designed by Sir D. Y.
Cameron.

April 1930.

CONTENTS

CHAPTER I

ILLUSTRATIONS

---

*The Frontispiece is from a photograph taken by Mr. Ian
Smith, Edinburgh, and the picture of the Union Gathering
is from a photograph taken by Mr. F. C. Inglis, Photographer
to H.M. the King at Edinburgh. The other two illustrations
are reproduced by the courtesy of Messrs. George Outram
& Co. Ltd., Glasgow.*

THE HISTORICAL BACKGROUND
OF UNION

CHAPTER I

THE HISTORICAL BACKGROUND OF UNION

THIS chapter is not an essay in Church history. History is an ampler thing which demands exact documentation and a multitude of details. It is no more than an attempt to sketch on the broadest lines the career of the Church in Scotland ; the vicissitudes which it suffered from controversies within and without its bounds ; the different strands interwoven in its creed ; the slow stages by which it attained to a clearer consciousness of its nature and its destiny.

I write as one who believes that that Church throughout its history was divinely inspired, and never in its darkest days ceased to fulfil in some degree its high mission.

But I believe, too, that, since it was also a human institution officered by fallible men, it blundered often, and had many needless years of sojourning in the wilderness. If the spark of celestial origin did not wholly die, other fires burned fiercely which were not divinely kindled. Yet it seems to me that we can discern a real continuity of growth. Slowly, very slowly, it discovered that comprehension was only possible if combined with tolerance. Through difficult stages it moved to a simplification of its confessions, and learned to distinguish essentials from " circumstantials." It became more clearly aware of the precise nature of its mission, and therefore of its proper relation to the civil government of the State. Without this steady simplifying and purifying process which its history reveals, the union of to-day would have been unthinkable. I am not of those who believe that true progress is ever attained by a straight and easy road, and beyond doubt the Church in Scotland has had to contend for every step of its advance. But it seems to me that, in spite of " right-hand snares and extremes and left-hand way-slidings," its story reveals, as in a spiral, a continuous upward movement.

There is no lack of literature on the subject, but the reader may find himself in trouble if he plunges without guidance into its mazes. Much of it is uncritical and unhistorical. The chronicle of the Scottish Church has too often been compiled in the spirit of hagiography. Some writers have approached it in a mood of rapt exaltation, and produced a device in snow and ink—spotless saints and infallible wisdom set against scowling diabolists and malignant folly. There has been no lack of casuists to defend the indefensible. It may be fairly said that history conceived in such a spirit does scant justice to the Church itself. On the other hand, it is easy for the cynic so to set forth its disputes as to make them seem the merest logomachies. The old divines write often uncouth English, and they are apt to make their arguments a mosaic of Scripture texts which lends itself readily to caricature. Causes for which men freely offered their lives can be made to seem trivial or ridiculous.

Of the two faults I think this the worse, for it is the less intelligent. The blindest hagiology seems to me preferable to that detachment which never comes within measurable distance of the point. Knox, Melville and Henderson—Boyd, Durham and Rutherford—Boston and the Erskines —Chalmers, Cunningham and Candlish— all were men of remarkable gifts of character and mind ; we may fairly assume that they did not give their time to wrangling about trifles ; it is our business to find out what kernel of living truth is concealed in a language which may have passed out of use. We must approach the historical Church with some equipment in the way of historical imagination, for even in its blunders we may find enlightenment. We cannot afford to look scornfully on any belief which once " taught weak wills how much they can." And there is this reward for the honest inquirer. Without some understanding of the Church there can be no true understanding of Scottish history or of the nature of the Scottish people.

I

The Mediaeval Church

The Church in Scotland has a long ancestry, but its descent is not in direct line. The Christian faith was first brought to our shores towards the end of the fourth century, when Ninian settled at Whithorn and built a great white church to the glory of God and the memory of St. Martin of Tours ; but soon the tides of war and paganism flowed over his work. In the middle of the sixth century Kentigern became the apostle of

Strathclyde, and, as St. Mungo, the patron saint of Glasgow. On Whit Sunday in the year 563 Columba landed in Iona, and he made that isle for the remaining thirty-four years of his life a light, the beams of which shone over all Scotland. We must give up, I fear, the pleasant tale derived from John of Fordun, of the early Scottish Church as being in substance Presbyterian and non-Roman. That Church was, like the Irish Church, monastic in its structure ; but as soon as it becomes an organised and national institution it is part of the catholic European system, though monastic elements, like the Culdees, long remain to testify to its beginnings.

It is as unhistorical to picture an early anti-papal Scottish Church as to imagine that the niceties of Roman rule were from the first universal, or that the Middle Ages knew only one uniform ecclesiastical pattern. There was nationalism in every Church ; most sovereigns had their quarrels with the

Pope, and many peoples lay occasionally under his ban. In Britain there was, perhaps, a special degree of spiritual independence. James I. of Scotland, a devout son of the Church, was as ready to assert himself against undue papal interference as William the Conqueror. The Scot, indeed, when he travelled abroad, carried with him a certain flavour of heterodoxy, and the validity of his orders was sometimes questioned. But in general we may say that the mediaeval Scottish Church was a normal branch of the Church Catholic whose centre was Rome.

It has been the fashion ever since the Reformation to picture that Church in dark colours, as something alien and despotic, with small hold on the affections of the people. The view has little warrant. The questioning spirit of the nation sometimes set the popular mind against its own hierarchy, and more often against the Roman Pontiff, for the Scot has always been more

individualist than catholic, and his aspira-
tion that of the old song :

> That all the world shall see
> There's nane right but we,
> The men of the auld Scottish nation.

But the mediaeval Church gave to the
people all of religion and humane learning
that they knew, and there is ample evidence
that it played, even in its decadence, a vital
part in men's lives. It produced the only
sacred poetry of the highest class that Scotland can claim. From the earliest days it
had its reformers and its evangelists as well
as its moderates. Even at the Reformation
the Christian virtues were not all on one side.
The great churchmen were often, like Lam-
berton and Wishart, leaders in the fight for
national independence. Henry Wardlaw
who founded the University of St. Andrews,
Kennedy who succeeded him in that see,
William Turnbull to whom we owe the
University of Glasgow, William Elphinstone

who was the creator of King's College at Aberdeen, must rank high amongst the benefactors of their country.

The Church which had endured for nearly a thousand years disappeared almost in a night, and with it went, unhappily, most of the outward evidence of its existence. Few ancient buildings remain still in use to remind us of that vanished world. But if we lack such memorials, we may claim an ultimate shrine. If the stream of Church history seems to be long lost among sands and morasses, we can recognise its fount. The little isle with its green hills and white beaches, which looks across the ribbon of tide to the granite of Mull, is a sacred place to which the devotion of every Scottish creed and communion is vowed. For there Columba, warrior, saint, scholar, explorer and law-giver, taught a simple evangel, first to the Gael and then to the other peoples of the mainland, and thereby lit the lamp of a missionary faith which has flickered often,

but has never died.   Iona is the Holy Land
and the Holy City of Scotland, the spring
of " the wisdom before which knowledge is
as a frosty breath."

II

THE FIRST REFORMATION

The Reformation came to Scotland in its
most drastic form.   There remained indeed
the same major articles of the Christian
faith, but, on grounds partly political and
partly religious, there was a final breach
with Rome, to some extent in creed and to
the full in ritual and Church government.
It began with the " Band " of December
1557, which denounced Roman abuses and
demanded the English Prayer-book : in
August 1560 a Confession of Faith, drawn
up by John Knox and his friends, was
ratified by Parliament as " wholesome and
sound doctrine grounded upon the infallible

truth of God's word " ; a few months later the first General Assembly was held, and the First Book of Discipline was approved ; and in the December Parliament of 1567, during the regency of Moray, the reformed Church was established by a statute " declaring and granting jurisdiction " to it, and disallowing " any other face of Kirk in Scotland."

The keynote of the Reformation was a return to simplicity. The great structure of the mediaeval Church, with its accretions of fifteen centuries, was exchanged for a simple revelation—God speaking through His Word to the individual heart and judgment. It claimed to replace an external standard by an internal, to be a re-birth of the spirit of man and a vindication of the liberties of the human soul. Its fundamental doctrine was the priesthood of all believers. Its conception of the Church was of a free autonomous community owning no leadership but that of Jesus Christ. But, since a human institution cannot be founded upon the bare principle of liberty, the new Church was at once compelled to seek definition and discipline.

The Reformation in its extremest, or, if we prefer, its purest form, was mainly the work of John Calvin, who performed two tasks of the first importance. In his *Institutes* he codified the theology of St. Augustine, and provided a body of doctrine, differing, indeed, only in emphasis from Catholic dogma, but skilfully adapted to the new conditions. In the Church which he founded at Geneva he created a model which Knox thought " the most perfect School of Christ that ever was on earth since the days of the Apostles," and which had a profound influence upon the nascent Church in Scotland.

But the hardening of the molten ore of spiritual fervour in the moulds of an institution was attended with certain difficulties, and, since in them is to be found the germ of all the later troubles of the

Scottish Church, it is necessary to examine them with some care.

The Basis of Faith

(1) The first concerned the basis of faith. The foundation of the Reformed Churches was the Bible ; they accepted no truth which had not a Scriptural warrant, and they claimed that whatever they did was done by Scripture authority. But the Bible must be interpreted, and the only means of interpretation, once the authority of an infallible Church had been rejected, was the human judgment and the human conscience. That remained the view of the more liberal among the Reformed theologians. " The authority of man," Hooker wrote, " is the key which openeth the door of entrance into the knowledge of the Scriptures."

But such a view inevitably involved diversity of opinion, and it seemed an insecure basis on which to build a lasting fabric.

Luther and Zwingli, for example, both founding upon the Bible, had reached different conclusions about the meaning of the Eucharist. Calvin and those who followed him saw the danger, and endeavoured to avoid it by something very like a return to the ecclesiasticism which he had rejected. We know, he held, that the Bible is the Word of God, not because of the authority of an historic Church, but because of the testimony of the Holy Spirit. This testimony must be systematised by God's servants, and a Church erected which shall be the medium of the Holy Spirit and the treasury of inspired interpretation. His *Institutes* in their second edition made definite claim to be the canon of Scripture teaching ; it was in his new Church and its accepted creed that saving knowledge could alone be found. This was not far from that doctrine of an external, infallible canon which the earlier Reformers had rejected.

Such an attitude towards the Bible and its

interpretation was a fruitful parent of strife. In the first place, it led to the most forced and arbitrary reading of Scripture texts. The Bible was made the sole manual of practice. The Church of Calvin and Knox forgot the warning of St. Paul—that the Old Testament was a dangerous book if the letter of it was regarded to the exclusion of the spirit, and it tended to make it a storehouse of minute precedents. The Roman Church had used for its basis not the Bible only, but the writings of the Fathers, and the dictates of practical experience, and it possessed the power of regulating the whole, and providing for natural development, by authoritative decree. The Scottish Church retained this doctrine of authority, but had somehow to harmonise it with a quantum of individual liberty, and it narrowed the canon to the two Testaments, thereby perilously limiting its tools.

At the beginning there was indeed a certain laxity. In 1558 the Scottish Protestants petitioned Mary of Guise that all matters might be tried by the New Testament, the ancient Fathers, and the " godly laws of Justinian." Knox, when it suited him, was prepared to differ even from the New Testament, and in an argument with Maitland of Lethington, who quoted St. James's direction to St. Paul to purify himself in the Temple, was bold enough to doubt " whether either James's command or Paul's obedience proceeded from the Holy Ghost." When Alexander Henderson disputed with Charles I., and the King argued that, when the Bible was not explicit, it was right to have recourse to the records of the Church, Henderson met him fairly on his own ground. But in general the early history of the Scottish Church shows a steady hardening and narrowing in its apologetics.

From this constriction of basis many misfortunes were to flow. The first was a perpetual risk of heresy and a constant invitation to schism. If ancient writings were to be construed without scientific method or historical perspective, it was certain that human ingenuity would find many causes of division. A second was the ossification of the minds engaged in so barren a task. The human reason in its worthier sense was atrophied by being limited to a futile casuistry. Superstitions, such as witchcraft and demoniac possession, were given by the idolatry of the Old Testament a new lease of life. The free use of the intellect was paralysed, and honest men become sophists. Ninian Winzet in his controversy with Knox had no difficulty in showing that the Reformers went to the Bible to find proofs for their creed, not to find that creed, since they rejected certain rules of the Roman Church which had scriptural warrant, and accepted others which had none. Andrew Melville based his objection to bishops on the ground that in the New Testament there was no mention of bishops ruling over presbyteries, ignoring the fact that his own system had just as little warrant, since there was no proof of a presbytery governing more than a single church.

In the following century the attitude became still more rigid. One Johann Koch of Leyden became, as Cocceius, anathema to the orthodox, because he held the reasonable view that Hebrew sentences should be interpreted by their context. Spiritually and intellectually this searching for proof-texts became a disease, for the truth in Donne's saying was ignored, that " sentences in Scripture, like hairs in horses' tails, concur in one root of beauty and strength, but, being plucked out one by one, serve only for springes and snares." Considerations of expediency and common sense were banned : the Bible was made a handbook to every aspect of life ; no word of the sacred writings but was regarded as dogma ; every syllable, letter, comma and full-stop was treated as divinely inspired : whatever was not contained therein was unlawful, for it was laid down as the first principle of interpretation that for God not to command was to forbid. And so we have Samuel Rutherford in his *Divine Right of Church Government and Excommunication* declaring that " there is nothing so small in either doctrinals or policy, so as man may alter, omit, or leave off these smallest positive things that God hath commanded."

This passionate formalism must obviously lead to credal divergencies, and it must inevitably land a Church in difficulties about rites and ceremonies. It was not easy to accommodate Christian worship in Western Europe in the sixteenth century to the practice of Judaean peasants in the first, or of Israel a thousand years earlier. The immediate result was confusion. The early Reformers in Scotland had no objection to settled forms and prescribed prayers. Knox began by accepting the kneeling posture at communion, though he afterwards rejected it. Wafer bread was employed by Calvin in his own church at Geneva. Winzet pointed out to Knox that there was no explicit warrant in the New Testament for either the baptism of infants or the strict observance of the Lord's Day. The first Reformers derived from the Church they had left a preference for a certain catholic order in worship until they were overborne by the Scripture literalists. This influence came chiefly from the English Puritans ; under their guidance Sunday, the day on which Calvin had played at bowls and Knox had given supper-parties, became the Jewish Sabbath, and selections from the Mosaic law were dovetailed into the Christian creed Even the ring in marriage would have been abolished had not the women proved stronger than the preachers.

The Conception of the Church

(2) If the seeds of dissension lay hidden in a basis of faith too narrow for the human

spirit, they were also present in the new conception of the Church. Presbytery, being
based on the Word of God, was a system
divini juris ; its founders were possessed by
the mediaeval idea of a universal Church ;
therefore we find it speedily claiming the
right to insist upon religious uniformity. It
was not only divinely founded, but, with its
Continental analogues, was the only system
of divine origin. It is easy to see how such
an attitude came about, for against the
universal claim of Rome it seemed necessary
to establish a counter-universalism. But it
involved two dangerous consequences—the
prohibition of variety in religious belief and
usage, and the duty of coercion. To the
Scottish Reformers it appeared that no
religion was safe unless it were predominant.

The new Church held firm by the Catholic
doctrine of comprehension, but it insisted
also upon uniformity—an apparently irre-
concilable ideal. The Church of Rome had
permitted within its pale all who formally

assented to its creed ; the Reformers tended to make the " church visible " also the " church invisible." The classic authority is the sixteenth chapter of Knox's *Confession* :

> " As we believe in one God, Father, Son and Holy Ghost, so do we most constantly believe that from the beginning there hath been, now is, and to the end of the world shall be, one Kirk ; that is to say, one company and multitude of men chosen of God, who rightly worship and embrace him by true faith in Christ Jesus . . . which kirk is Catholic, that is, universal, because it containeth the elect of all realms, nations and tongues. And we utterly abhor the blasphemy of those that affirm that men which live according to equity and justice shall be saved, what religion soever they have professed."

The practical doctrine, adumbrated by Knox and made explicit by his successors, was that it was God's will that the Kirk, which was scripturally the only true Kirk, should admit no rival in any sphere where it had won dominance, and should suffer no

internal divergencies from its divinely-in-
spired interpretation of Scriptural mandates.
It believed, as Rome believed, in the ideal
of a single Church, a complete and exclusive
system to which a single separatist was
anathema.

From such a conception the duty of
coercion inevitably followed. Our Lord
never taught the exercise of coercive power,
and the early Church was not in a position
to attempt it. But in the fourth century,
with the acknowledgment of Christianity as
the State religion, the practice began ;
heresy became treason ; and St. Augustine,
building on the isolated text, " Compel them
to come in," preached the use of force in
conversion. The view was based upon his
doctrine of the utter depravity of the natural
man, since, if human nature was hopelessly
corrupt, there was no reason to consult its
wishes. " What can be more deadly to the
soul," he asked, " than the liberty of error ? "
" Toleration," said Richard Baxter in the

seventeenth century, " is soul murder." The view was inevitable, granted the premises, for on them tolerance seemed no better than spiritual sloth and moral apathy. This was the belief alike of Protestant and Catholic, of Knox and of Innocent III., of Andrew Melville and of the Cardinal of Lorraine. A man like Samuel Rutherford, who was what was commonly known as an " affectionate " preacher, taught, as has been said, " the loveliness of Christ for thirty years without ever perceiving the unloveliness of intolerance."

Another consequence was the institution of a drastic internal discipline, in order that the visible might be made to approximate as far as possible to the invisible Church. Evidence, indeed, could not be demanded of the possession of saving grace, but over every outward manifestation there was exercised a minute inquisition. No serious attempt was made to distinguish between moral fundamentals and non-fundamentals, and the most secular aspects of life were not exempted from oversight. Once again the conclusion followed logically from certain dubious premises. Historically we can perceive its justification, but in its results it was disastrous. " By your hard and subtle words," Cromwell was to tell the ministers before Dunbar, " you have begotten prejudice in those who do too much in matters of conscience—wherein every soul has to answer for itself to God—depend upon you " ; and the indictment was unhappily true.

The Relation to the Civil Power

(3) The third potential source of strife was the relation to the civil power. Ever since Constantine this problem had confronted the Church, and the great *Corpus Juris* of Justinian defined the respective rights of Church and State—a definition at first accepted by the Reformers. Presently their attitude changed. Hag-ridden by Old

Testament precedents, they came to believe
that the visible sign of God's acknowledgment of His people was the gift of political
power.   The Church was not only supreme
in spiritual matters, but it was the duty of a
Christian State to support it and to lend the
secular arm, when required, to carry out its
decrees, to punish heresy and enforce discipline, and to suppress any Church which
threatened rivalry.   In the fathers of Presbytery there was nothing of the *politique*
whose creed has been defined by Tavannes :
" Ceux qui preférent le repos du royaume,
ou de leur particulier, au salut de leur âme,
et à la religion, qui ayment mieux que le
royaume demeure en paix sans Dieu qu'en
guerre pour luy." [1]

This view involved the Church's establishment, and Knox and Melville and Henderson were Erastians in one sense of that
doubtful word.   Moreover, the rejection of
toleration and the belief in uniformity were

[1] *Mémoires*, ed. Buchon, 269.

bound to lead to a usurpation of civil power. With such a creed there could be no real delimitation between the spiritual and the secular, between Church and State. The right of the Church to dominate personal and family life was soon extended to the duty of interference with secular government. Its maxim became *Cujus religio, ejus regio*, the converse of the mediaeval formula. Doubtless it is true, as has been argued, that the original aim, as shown by the use of the phrase the " crown honours of Christ," was less to aggrandise the Church than to exalt the majesty of our Lord. But in fact it was soon to develop into a claim which was inconsistent with any stable civil society.

Of this fatal heritage of the Middle Ages Knox was the chief exponent. The Reformation in Scotland was largely political, the work of laymen ; its most effective champions, the nobles, owed their bitterness against Rome mainly to the desire to retain Church lands ; so the relationship with the

civil power was from the start a vital issue.
Knox—*clarum et venerabile nomen*—one of the
greatest destructive forces in our history and
no mean constructive one, had immense
shrewdness and practical wisdom, but he had
little power of coherent thought.   He is one
of the most inconsistent of writers and
speakers, and his mind is constantly in a
passionate confusion.   From such a man it
was idle to expect any wise and cogent
definition of the respective powers of State
and Church.   It was owing to him that the
Reformation in Scotland went so deep ; but
if he left his country the bequest of a noble
democracy, he left it also a tradition of
rigidity and intolerance and political strife.

For the essence of his conception of the
Church was really that of unlimited authority.   It could not choose but interfere in
civil affairs.   There was no agreement on
what constituted an ecclesiastical offence ;
an Edinburgh elder, for example, was
ordered to do penance in the kirk for ex-

porting wheat. Andrew Melville's famous declaration about the two kings and two kingdoms in Scotland might seem a reasonable statement of spiritual independence, but its occasion was a claim of the ministers to interfere in secular policy.[1] In theory, the Church professed to separate civil and ecclesiastical jurisdiction with scrupulous care, and it always objected to ecclesiastics holding civil offices ; but in fact no barrier could long stand, the Church's claims being what they were. The doctrine of the Headship of Christ was interpreted in the long run so as to overrule all lesser sanctions. That was the true root of the trouble over Episcopacy, and not a mere difference in the reading of certain New Testament passages. The Kings, James and Charles, desired a hierarchy so as to give them more control over the Church ; the Church desired the liberty of extending, when it so desired, its spiritual prerogatives into secular domains.

[1] Rait, *The Parliaments of Scotland*, 53.

Both based their arguments on divine right. It was a conflict of rival extremes.

III

PRESBYTERY AND EPISCOPACY

With high purpose and a sincere devotion, but with those perilous elements, which we have sketched, in its constitution, the Reformed Church of Scotland started upon its journey. It had come into being by its own act, independent of the civil power, for its birth was the General Assembly of 1560-61. At that date the national Church sprang into life ; seven years later an Act of Parliament made it an established Church ; that is to say, the State did not create the Church's authority, but recognised formally that which was already existing. Its organisation, its ritual, and even its doctrines were not yet wholly settled, but its spiritual autonomy was indisputable, since it owned no headship but Christ's.

It began in 1560 with a purely administrative Episcopacy, not possessed of orders higher than those of the ordinary ministry. The superintendents, or bishops, were subject to the control of the General Assembly, and the main purpose of their office was to perform the duties of local administration, which, under the influence of Andrew Melville, were, about 1580, assigned to the newly-instituted Church courts, known as presbyteries. The position, however, see-sawed according to the prestige of the King at the moment, for James did not admit the Church's claim of spiritual autonomy, and regarded an hierarchy as a necessary protection for the throne. In 1584 the Black Acts recognised the King as the head of the Church, and made the meetings of the General Assembly depend upon the permission of King and Parliament ; in 1592 the position was reversed, and a complete Presbyterian polity was established ; by 1600 James had triumphed again and

c

bishops sat in Parliament. When he succeeded to the English throne he won a new
authority, the Act of 1592 was repealed, and
Episcopacy became the law. In the same
way the Articles of Perth, ratified by Parliament in 1621, made customs approximate to
the English rather than to the Genevan code,
by enjoining kneeling at communion, con-
firmation, and the keeping of certain Church
festivals.

But neither the parliamentary Episcopacy
nor the Perth Articles greatly affected the
life of the Church, for the law was not
strictly enforced, and James had the wisdom
to call a halt in his policy of religious
uniformity. The discipline and practice
were in substance Presbyterian, especially as
regards local government. The General
Assembly lost first its authority and then its
existence, and the bishops exercised such
political influence as remained to the Church.
Their political power encouraged among
their opponents that tendency by which

the Church, under the inspiration of the
Melvilles, came to regard itself more
and more as a self-governing commonwealth, wholly independent in all things
which by any stretch of language could be
called spiritual. Knox had written : " The
ordering and reformation of religion doth
especially appertain to the Civil Magistrate.
. . . The King taketh upon him to command the Priests." By 1620 no leader of
Presbytery in Scotland but would have re-
pudiated this dictum of its founder.

Yet in the first decades of the seventeenth
century there was no final bar to uniformity
between England and Scotland. The new
impulse in religion had first come north of
Tweed through the study of Wycliffe's Bible,
and both nations had the Word of God in
the same tongue. There was some justification for James's policy. Both Churches
were Protestant and Calvinist ; both had
liturgies which might have been made one
had the advice of John Hales been followed,

and a public form of service devised embracing only those things upon which all Christians were agreed.[1] There was an opportunity for a true eirenicon, as Archbishop Ussher believed, if bishops were required to follow the primitive practice and act on the advice of the ministers, laymen were brought into church management, and churchmen were disqualified for civil office. There was a real chance of union under James ; under Charles I. it vanished, and has not returned.

Episcopacy, in the attenuated form in which it had been now established, might well have been tolerated in spite of Andrew Melville's theoretic objections, since it bore so lightly on the ordinary man. It had not much prestige—the *tulchan* bishops had seen to that—but it roused no great antipathy, and it interfered little with Presbyterian usage. The trouble which began under Charles I. was due not to Episcopacy but

---

[1] See his *Tract concerning Schisme*, 1642.

to Prelacy. " Episcopacy," Sir Thomas Raleigh has written, " is a form of government, possessing a strong claim upon our respect and gratitude. Prelacy is a vice, and a vice which is not peculiar to the episcopal churches. It makes its appearance wherever a minister of the Word imagines that his office entitles him to exercise lordship over his brethren. It was in the Church from the first ; for we remember how the companions of Christ disputed which of them should be greatest, and how Salome asked that her son should have the chief place in the Kingdom." [1] The prelate, as " one set above," was an offence to a Church which believed in the parity of ministers, and for the King to claim to alter ritual and interfere with Church government of his own will was to undermine the spiritual freedom which was the Church's chief foundation.

[1] *Annals of the Church in Scotland*, 10.

The Second Reformation

So we reach what is sometimes known as the Second Reformation, which was a revolt from Prelacy, as the First Reformation had been a revolt from Rome. Charles i. by his revocation of Church property in the hands of laymen had alarmed the nobles and barons, and thereby provided for the Church in her disputes a new set of Lords of the Congregation. He had established a court of High Commission, increased the number of bishops in the Privy Council to seven, and made Archbishop Spottiswoode Chancellor —the first time since the Reformation that the office had been given to a churchman. He passed from one blunder to another, driving even royalists like Drummond of Hawthornden into opposition, till in 1637 he imposed, by an act of pure autocracy, a new Prayer-book upon the Scottish Church. The result was to fire the heather and to unite all Scotland against him, except a few

Catholic nobles and Aberdeen doctors. The National Covenant was signed in the first months of 1638, a temperate and strictly legal assertion of the autonomy of the national Church. In November of the same year a General Assembly held at Glasgow, formally illegal, but with a solid nation behind it, decreed a root-and-branch abolition of Episcopacy and its ministrants.

It would have been well had the Church been content to stop there. With all the irregularities of its procedure, it had required that Scottish liberties should be safeguarded, and demanded in proof the grant of the kind of Church which the nation preferred. In its insistence upon spiritual freedom it had ample historical warrant. But the dangerous constituents in its heritage were now to come uppermost, and too many of its leaders had the vision of Hildebrand in their souls and the spirit of Hildebrand in their blood. It is a hazardous thing to claim that any system of church government is *divini juris*, unless it be granted that the claim can be shared among many systems. " Establish," said Coleman, preaching before the House of Commons in July 1645, " as few things by divine right as can well be." The claim to possess a monopoly of divine inspiration came from a casuistical and unscholarly interpretation of the Scriptures, and on the same basis Independent, Quaker, and Laudian Anglican could reach the same conclusion about his own belief. Of such, a premise uniformity was the logical consequence, and to insist upon it became a duty. This was the creed as much of Henderson and Guthrie as of Laud and Charles. " In the paradise of Nature," wrote Henderson in 1640, " the diversity of flowers and herbs is pleasant and useful, but in the paradise of the Church different and contrary religions are unpleasant and hurtful." Note that " different " and " contrary " were conjoined. Scotland claimed to dictate to England her ecclesiastical polity.

There was nobility in the dream, but it was a noble folly. The Scottish divines had never lost the vision of a single catholic and universal Church upon earth. You will find it in Melville and Brown of Wamphray; you will find it in Samuel Rutherford and James Durham, as well as in Archbishop Leighton. They never unchurched their old enemy Rome, or treated her baptism as invalid. They were always unwilling separatists, and longed for reunion—on their own terms. Durham is vehement against the divisions " occasioned by a carnal and factious-like pleading for and vindicating even of truth." They had a horror of light-hearted schism and a pathetic desire to see Christ's people in concord. Durham's congested style becomes on this subject almost eloquent :

> " Never did men run to quench fire in a city, lest all should be destroyed, with more diligence than men ought to bestir themselves to quench this in the Church. Never did mariners use

more speed to stop a leak in a ship, lest all should be drowned, than ministers especially and all Christian men should haste to stop this beginning of the breaking in of these waters of strife, lest thereby the whole Church be overwhelmed.   And if the many evils which follow therefrom, the many commands whereby union is pressed, yea, the many entreaties and obtestations whereby the Holy Ghost doth so frequently urge this upon us all, as a thing most acceptable to Him and profitable to us—if, I say, these and many other considerations have not weight to convince of the necessity of this duty to prevent or heal a breach, we cannot tell what can prevail with men that profess reverence to the great and dreadful name of God, conscience of duty, and respect to the edification of the Church, and to their own peace at the appearance of the Lord in the great day, wherein the peacemakers shall be blessed, for they shall be called the children of God." [1]

But so long as there was no clear distinction between the essential and the inessential, so long as unity was identified with uniformity, this passionate desire for union became an

[1] *Treatise concerning Scandal* (1659), 313.

explosive to shatter instead of a cement
to bind.

The result was the Solemn League and
Covenant, signed in St. Margaret's Church,
Westminster, in September 1643, and there-
after sworn to by the Estates and the General
Assembly and the Scottish people, in which
the Church violently encroached upon the
sphere of secular government. It was regarded as a mystical covenant with the
Almighty, its acceptance a test of faith, its
rejection or breach a certain proof of damna-
tion. This method of covenant-making was
a lamentable descent into a legal formalism
which degraded the whole conception of the
relationship of God and His people. It had
immediate and disastrous results. It set
Scotland in sharp antagonism to a large part
of the people of England ; it drove from the
Scottish Church the greatest of its sons,
Montrose ; it intensified the spirit of sectarian bigotry into which it was drifting ; it
earned the hearty enmity of the foremost of

Englishmen, and of all those who, like Cromwell, were striving for toleration. But the labours of the divines at Westminster, the sponsors of the Solemn League, brought forth one worthy fruit. They produced an ordinal of public worship, and they codified their theology in the Confession of Faith, which has remained ever since in substance the doctrinal base of Scottish Presbytery.

The Restoration

The rule of Cromwell in Scotland meant the practical curbing of the theocracy into which the Church had drifted. The Restoration of 1660 meant the upturning of its foundations. The Church, having sought too much, was now to get less than its due, and that spiritual liberty which in its pride it had denied to others was now to be denied to itself. Just as the Glasgow Assembly of 1638 had abolished James's laws, so the Act Rescissory of 1661 blotted out twenty-three years of Presbyterian legislation. The restored Episcopacy resembled that of the reign of James rather than the Laudian ideal of uniformity with England. But it was the King who dictated the Church's constitution ; Episcopacy had become identified with the loss of liberty, and the issue was now not as to the merits or demerits of a form of government but as to whether the Church's autonomy was to be maintained. The Headship of Christ became the testing question. Most of Scotland, being very weary, settled down under the new regime, but in the south and west the flower of the ministers and laymen opposed the King. There was dross as well as fine gold in such men. The strife was largely one of rival intolerances, and the Covenanters held as firmly as Laud ever did to the principle of uniformity. They would have had all men compelled to adopt a single creed and practice, but that creed and practice must be their own. Yet they fought

blindly and confusedly for one lasting truth,
the Church's spiritual freedom, and, if only
for their testimony on that behalf, they
deserve to be held in honourable memory.

The Revolution of 1688 saw the close of
the second great stage in the Church's history. That stage began with the Second Reformation when Prelacy was overthrown and
the freedom of the Church was vindicated ;
it ended with the Church in servitude to the
civil authority, a lack-lustre nominal Episcopacy, and some of the best of the Scottish
people outlaws for conscience sake. More
serious still, the habit of separatism had
grown, and the seamless robe of the Church
was rent asunder. The quarrels of Resolu-
tioner and Protester had been followed after
the Restoration by the Covenanting breach,
and the Covenanters themselves threatened
to split up into lesser conventicles—" a
poor, wasted, misrepresented Remnant," in
the words of James Renwick's *Informatory
Vindication*, " of the Suffering, Anti-Popish,

Anti-Prelatic, Anti-Erastian, Anti-Sectarian, true Presbyterian Church of Christ in Scotland."

Yet throughout that troubled age an ideal of a Church at peace with itself was never forgotten, and there is often more wisdom to be got from the writings of the divines than from their public utterances and actions. The ferment of the time produced many men of real, if one-sided, greatness. There were fervid evangelists who made a fire in cold places ; scholars and thinkers like Robert Boyd and James Durham and Brown of Wamphray ; mystics like Samuel Rutherford, whose saccharine sweetness often cloys, but who can rise now and then to an apocalyptic splendour ; quaint souls like William Guthrie of Fenwick—a Scottish Traherne or Henry Vaughan—who bade his hearers praise God, " if ye have no more, for this good day and sunshine to the lambs" [1] ; Leighton, a bishop of the Restora-

[1] Wodrow, *Analecta*, I. 137.

tion Episcopacy, whose sermons were Coleridge's delight, and who laboured for peace where peace could not be ; James Renwick, the last martyr, a man of wistful apostolic power. Most of them died young, worn out with an eternal dissidence, for they had to build God's house, like Nehemiah, with trowel in one hand and sword in the other. One and all they were men of a noble fortitude, confused sometimes and a little blind, but of a great stoutness of heart. In that age of suffering and darkness their eyes were always on the world beyond time, and often, in their too ardent contemplation of immortality, they were careless of mortal wisdom and the humbler mortal duties. Each " fired his ringing shot and passed " to the rest for which he was always longing. Their words were those of Cromwell—" We are indeed but a feeble and sickly company, yet we shall work the time that is appointed us, and after that rest in peace."

IV

THE REVOLUTION SETTLEMENT

The Revolution Settlement—mainly the work of William Carstares, who must rank high among ecclesiastical statesmen—was a peace of exhaustion. The fact that the Scottish bishops took the side of James made it certain that Episcopacy would disappear from the national Church. For the rest, Presbytery was established, patronage was abolished, and the Confession of Faith was made statute law. It seemed that the Church had been confirmed in its exclusive spiritual jurisdiction and its intrinsic spiritual powers. There was no mention of Covenants, or of the theocratic claims which had begun with the Glasgow Assembly of 1638 ; it was as if it had been tacitly agreed that that stormy chapter should be forgotten.

From this fatigued unanimity there were two main dissentients. Many of the Epis-

D

copalian clergy to their honour followed the
King, whose divine right to the throne had
been part of their creed. They paid the
price of their loyalty, and the sufferings of
those Scottish non-jurors are too often forgotten. There was justification for Pley-
dell's epithet for the communion to which
he belonged—" the persecuted Episcopal
Church of Scotland." [1] But in certain districts in the north, where that Church had a
large popular following, the old regime continued undisturbed.   It differed from that of
Presbytery only in its acceptance of bishops,
and in its attitude towards the reigning
house.   Its ritual was of the simplest, it
celebrated communion according to the
barest Presbyterian fashions, and its creed
was indistinguishable from that laid down
in the Confession of Faith.

The other dissentients were to be found in
the south-west, the men of the Societies, who
followed the blood-reddened banner of

[1] In *Guy Mannering*.

Richard Cameron and Donald Cargill. They claimed to be the historic Church of Scotland, compelled through the errors of the majority to withdraw themselves into private societies for Christian fellowship. For a decade or two they led a stormy life, lit by political intrigues ; the Jacobites regarded them as likely allies, and their dealings with the Society men may be read in the unedifying pages of Ker of Kersland. The Cameronians held strictly to the Covenants, and could not acknow- ledge an uncovenanted Kirk or an un- covenanted King. By and by, through the work of men like John M'Millan of Bal- maghie, the Societies were organised into a Presbytery, which ultimately became a Church—the Reformed Presbyterian Church of Scotland, the first and not the least estim- able of Scottish secessions.

In 1712, by a mischievous trick of the English Tories and the Scottish Jacobites, patronage was restored, and the dragon's teeth were sown which were to produce a melancholy harvest. The Church protested against it, but for a little it was no great grievance, since ministers continued to be placed by the will of a congregation rather than by the nomination of a patron. But presently the patrons became more active, presbyteries refused to give assent to their wishes, and the General Assemblies were congested with appeals. The device of peripatetic " riding committees," sent abroad to settle disputes, was a solution which had no hope of permanence. Here was one rock of offence, the more dangerous because certain younger ecclesiastics, who were afterwards to be leaders of the Moderates, were anxious in this matter to make the Assembly dictate harshly to the presbyteries.

Another was the inclination to heresy hunts, a danger in all churches which have no strong spiritual inspiration. In 1695 Thomas Aikenhead, a lad of nineteen, who favoured a fantastic materialism and considered the Pentateuch to be post-Exilian, was tried and condemned. He recanted—which would have saved his life at the hands of the Inquisition—but was duly hanged in Edinburgh. Soon controversies arose in the inner circles of the orthodox. A century before, a certain fellow of Brasenose College, Oxford, had published a book called *The Marrow of Modern Divinity*, in which the doctrine of saving grace was stated in its extreme Calvinistic form. This ancient work was seized upon by those ministers who scented latitudinarian tendencies, and the " Marrow-men " became a dangerous left wing in the Church, trembling upon the brink of secession.

The Secessions

The result was an exemplification of that characteristic which Thomas Hobbes had long ago marked in Presbyterianism, a lia-

bility to hive off into sects. The first schism
was that of the Erskines, who had been
Marrow-men along with Boston of Ettrick ;
the ostensible ground was patronage and
the growing Erastian character of the
Church, though doctrinal dissatisfaction also
played a part ; they had never accepted
the Revolution Settlement, and were still
harking back upon the Covenants like the
old Protesters.[1] " There is a difference
to be made," wrote Ebenezer Erskine,
" between the Established Church of Scotland and the Church of Christ in Scotland " ;
and he proceeded to constitute the latter as
a secession Church. That was in 1733, and
twelve years later there was a secession
within this secession. It turned on the
validity of the burgess oath—whether one
could conscientiously swear to uphold " the
true religion presently professed within this
realm." Those who maintained that the

[1] Cf. Lord Sands' paper in *Records of the Scottish Church
History Society*, 1928.

establishment was corrupt could scarcely approve such a form of words. So the first secession split into Burgher and Anti-Burgher, and half a century later the former split again into New Lights and Old Lights, according to the degree of modernism among its members. The same division showed itself among the Anti-Burghers, the eternal dichotomy of conservatives and progressives. The basis was partly doctrinal, but far more that old rock of Scottish controversy, the relation of Church and State.

There was still a third hiving-off in 1761, in the Relief Church, whose founder was Thomas Gillespie, and which had a more liberal character than its predecessors. The brethren of the Relief had no enthusiasm for the letter of the Covenants. " I do not think," wrote Patrick Hutchison, " that ever any part of the Church of Christ, since the commencement of the Christian era, was more deeply involved in the guilt of ignorant and false swearing than the British

subjects in the last century." [1]   They held,
too, by comprehensive communion, for their
synod in 1773 declared : " It is agreeable
to the Word of God and their principles
occasionally to hold communion with those of
the Episcopal and Independent persuasions
who are visible saints."

Moderatism

The various secessions profoundly weakened the Church of Scotland by withdrawing
from it many men of true religious genius.
The ranks of the establishment closed up in
a dry and formal unity against a menace
which was real enough, for by 1766 there
were 120 secession meeting-houses attended
by more than 100,000 worshippers.   The
consequence was the Moderatism which for
more than a century was the dominant policy
of the Church.   The Moderates had many

[1] *Compendious View of the Religious System of the Synod of
Relief*, 1779.

merits, and it is as unfair to judge them by a pagan like " Jupiter " Carlyle, as it would be to judge their opponents, the High-flyers, by Dr. Webster of the Tolbooth Church, the " Dr. Magnum Bonum " of many tales, who had the bad taste to complain that while he drank with gentlemen he must vote with fools. A man like William Robertson, the historian and Principal of Edinburgh University, was as orthodox in theology as any seceder, and far more liberal and tolerant. The party did a useful work in lowering the temperature in ecclesiastical controversy, and loosening the bonds of antiquarian dogmas.

But none the less they were a chilling influence in Scotland. The piety of their devout men—and they had many—was apt to be without fervour, and so without popular appeal. Their clergy were aloof from their parishioners, and inclined, under the blight of patronage, to be subservient to the local gentry. They had their own

intolerances. If they were free on the whole
from what Melancthon called the *rabies
theologorum*, they had a stiff legalism not less
distasteful. They were hostile to all missionary and evangelical effort, and Chalmers'
summary was not untrue of the majority :

> " A morality without godliness, a certain
> prettiness of sentiment served up in tasteful and
> well-turned periods of composition—the ethics
> of philosophy or of the academic chair rather
> than the ethics of the Gospel, the speculations
> of natural theology, or, perhaps, an ingenious
> and scholarlike exposition of the credentials,
> rather than a faithful exposition of the contents
> of the New Testament ; these, for a time, dis-
> possessed the topics of other days, and occupied
> that room in our pulpits which had formerly
> been given to the demonstration of sin and the
> Saviour."

A religion without enthusiasm is a religion
without life and without hope of growth.
Also, this enlightenment had its childish side.
The ministers who thronged to the perform-
ance of Home's *Douglas*, and flocked after

Mrs. Siddons, and made a parade of their little liberties, have to me an indescribable air of naughty urchins.

But Moderatism, great as were its defects, made its own contribution to the development of Church and nation. It meant the abandonment for good and all of the fantastic theocratic dreams of the previous century. It was a disintegrating force when brought to bear on certain debasing superstitions. The Church, for all the dialectical power of its theology, had been slow to apply the same vigour of mind to the examination of witchcraft and cognate beliefs, and as late as 1697 we have the amazing case of Christian Shaw of Bargarran, who was tormented by devils, a story which carries us back to the heart of the Middle Ages. Good men like Wodrow and bad men like Lord Grange were alike opposed to a relaxation of the savage witchcraft laws. But, as the eighteenth century advanced, the light of common-sense began to penetrate the darkness, and we find Mr. Fraser of Tiree and Mr. Campbell of Aberfeldy treating " Satan's invisible world " as a subject for cool scientific inquiry.   Hutcheson's lectures on moral philosophy at Glasgow prepared the way for that *Aufklärung* which, however shallow its inspiration, was at any rate the foe of the blinder superstitions.

Let it not be forgotten that it is to the Moderates that we owe an infusion of the rationalistic spirit, " sapping a solemn creed with solemn sneer," which is an ingredient in all progress.   It was the only path to toleration, since, as Charles James Fox once said, for toleration there is needed a certain degree of honest scepticism.   Behind all their cant and foppery there was this solid achievement—the provision of the necessary sceptical dissolvent for belated or perverse dogmas. They preached the forgotten lesson of the importance of the human reason in all human endeavour, and they strove to link religion to those other spheres of intellectual effort

from which it had too long been divorced.
Without the help of this uninspired and
matter-of-fact sagacity Scotland would have
been slow to clear her feet of mediaeval
lumber. Theirs was the same spirit which
in the secular world made her turn her back
upon vain dreams of separation and revolt
and work out for herself her economic
salvation.

It is a mistake, I think, to regard the
ecclesiastical life of the capital city in the
eighteenth century as truly reflecting the
religious life of Scotland. The ministers
satirised by Burns had no doubt their
counterparts in most shires, " cauld har-
angues " were varied by the " Gospel club,"
and the hungry sheep were fed now with
a drab morality, now with superheated
imaginings, and now with barren scholastic
subtleties. But the records of kirk sessions
and presbyteries show us that the plain
evangel was widely taught by wise and
simple preachers. Survivals of the old, stern

tradition of the saints kept the spiritual
fires alight, even within the Church, and
most Lowland parishes could boast a David
Deans or a Gifted Gilfillan. The central
Borders had shared less than many districts
in the Covenanting fervours, but we may
read in James Hogg how real a thing religion
was in the life of the Border peasant. He
made the Bible the lamp of his path, and at
family prayers communed fearlessly with his
Maker. " The flocks on a thousand hills
are Thine and their lives and death wad be
naething to Thee. Thou wad naither be
the richer nor the poorer, but, oh Lord, it 's
a great matter to huz." Nor was the spirit
of critical independence absent, and he was
under no blind bondage to the letter of the
Word. The householder would stop his
reading of the Bible with the remark : " If
it hadna been the Lord's will, that verse had
been better left out." We have already
travelled far from Samuel Rutherford.

The End of the Century

With the end of the eighteenth century came the dawning of a new world. The *Aufklärung* gave place, in literature, to the Romantic Revival. Robert Burns interpreted Scotsmen to one another and wove into one poetic tradition the conflicting strains in our history. Sir Walter Scott revealed his country to itself and to the world. Scotland had set her house in order, her industries were entering upon an era of wide expansion, and her agriculture was rapidly becoming a model to all Britain. Political thought, stimulated by the French Revolution, was no longer content with a museum piece like the Scottish system of representation, and doctrines were professed by reputable citizens which would have sent their fathers to the gallows. Of this stirring in men's minds there were two main consequences. Scotland's nationalism was intensified, and her pride enlarged ; she was resolved to hold by her past as well as to march boldly towards the future. Again, the critical spirit was abroad, and it was certain that no doctrine or institution would be long exempt from it.

The century closed with an established Church in uneasy alliance with the State, and a number of secession churches, free indeed from such entanglements, but shackled with heavy dogmatic bonds. Some of the old matters of dispute had been shed. Prelacy would never again interfere with Presbytery, and the removal of its disabilities in 1792 enabled the Scottish Episcopal Church to follow its own natural development. The Covenants were no longer a dead hand, even in the sects which had left the parent Church because of them. There was a movement towards a more liberal construction of the Creed, and wise men were beginning to hold the true Reformation view—that a living Church must be free to change its confessions within the wide limits of the Scripture faith. In the Church of Scotland itself the State establishment was a cardinal principle, but it had lost the dangerous rider which the seventeenth century had given it ; if it still based itself on the text in Isaiah, " Kings shall be thy nursing fathers and queens thy nursing mothers," it did not press the second clause of the verse, " They shall bow down to thee with their faces towards the earth and lick up the dust of thy feet." Indeed, the Church's pretensions as regards the State had become humility itself, and patronage tended to make it a disconsidered dependent.

Yet in the minds of many there was a vision of a national religion, " the restoration," in Montrose's words, " of that which our first Reformers had." Among the seceders there was little valuing of secession for its own sake, and some of their leaders were beginning to dream of an eventual unity. And in all the various kirks there was growing up a conception of what

E

Presbytery might yet become, a faith of which Principal Rainy, in his reply to Dean Stanley, has given a classic definition :

" Presbyterianism meant organised life, regulated distribution of forces, graduated recognition of gifts, freedom to discuss, authority to control, agency to administer. Presbyterianism meant a system by which the convictions and conscience of the Church could constantly be applied, by appropriate organs, to her current affairs. Presbyterianism meant a system by which quickening influence, experienced anywhere in the Church, could be turned into effective form and transmitted to fortify the whole society. Presbyterianism meant a system by which any one, first of all the common man, had his recognised place, his defined position, his ascertained and guarded privileges, his responsibilities inculcated and enforced, felt himself a part of the great unity, with a right to care for its welfare and to guard its integrity. From the broad base of the believing people, the sap rose through Sessions, Presbyteries, Synods, to the Assembly, and, thence descending, diffused knowledge, influence, unanimity through the whole system.

Presbyterianism is a system for a free people that love a regulated, a self-regulating freedom."

It was a great ideal, which still awaits its full accomplishment.

V

THE MOVEMENT TOWARDS REFORM

The nineteenth century was to see at once a movement towards union and a further disruption, for much had to be pulled down before a new and ampler building could arise. Scotland, for the better part of a hundred years, was filled with controversy, which, if less bitter and more fruitful than that of the seventeenth century, was scarcely less vehement and continuous. To the detached observer it seemed that the land was spending its strength in barren debate. In an " Appeal to the Clergy of the Church of Scotland," published in 1875, Robert Louis Stevenson wrote :—" It would be difficult to exaggerate the pity that fills my heart at such a reflection ; at the thought of how this neck of barren hills between two inclement seaways has echoed for three centuries with the uproar of sectarian battles ; of how the east wind has carried out the sound of our shrill disputation into the desolate Atlantic, and the west wind has borne it over the German Ocean, as though it would make all Europe privy to how well we Scottish brethren abide together in unity. It is not a bright page in the annals of a small country." Yet it is hard to see how this epoch of controversy could have been avoided, though it might well have been curtailed. There were in dispute matters of moment which were capable of no easy solution, but for which a solution must be found if the Church in Scotland was to fulfil its mission.

During the first decades of the century there were stirrings of life in many quarters. Men like Erskine of Linlathen and M'Leod

Campbell were feeling their way towards a more liberal theology. An evangelical movement, which may be said to represent in Scotland the ultimate ripples of the great tidal wave of Wesley's work in England, was putting life into the dry bones of orthodoxy. In the Highlands especially, the " Men," prophets of an antique stamp, brought to the preaching of the Gospel the passion and mysticism of the Celt. In the secession Churches scholars were arising, like Robertson of Irvine and John Cairns, who illuminated Scottish divinity with a scholarship drawn from France and Germany. Missionary enterprise was beginning—in India under Alexander Duff, in South Africa under David Livingstone and Robert Moffat.

But, for the rest, the rule of the past was strictly obeyed. Church architecture retained its pristine hideousness. A Scottish service followed the meagre Puritan fashion —not that of the first Reformers—and was in the main a lengthy monologue by the preacher. Patronage lay heavy on the Church, and the dominant Moderate party were stiff legalists both in doctrine and practice. In dogma they held by the letter of the Westminster Confession ; in ecclesiastical policy they inclined to emphasise the dependence of the Church upon the civil law. Their conservatism was less a political creed than a temperamental bias, for they held, like Lady Rachel Drummond, that " a new light could enter only through a crack either in the head or in the heart." They were, in Lord Cockburn's phrase, that inexorable type of revolutionary " which will change nothing voluntarily, and thus compels everything to change itself forcibly."

As the century advanced the new forces gathered strength, and it was very clear that ere long there must be conflict. The new wine was too strong for the old bottles. The example of the secession Churches made it certain that the issue would be joined upon patronage. The majority of the reform

party were on the progressive side in politics, but their leader, Thomas Chalmers,
was a staunch Conservative, who professed
a " moral loathing " for the Whigs. In the
Assembly of 1832, under his Moderatorship,
the question was raised of a popular veto
upon the nomination of a patron. One
suggestion was that the Legislature should be
petitioned to abolish patronage, a course
which might well have succeeded ; but the
predominant view was that the Church
itself should legislate on the matter. The
consequence was the passing in 1834 of a
Veto Act, which laid down that a majority
of the male heads of households, being com-
municants, were empowered to veto a pre-
sentation. At the same time the question
was raised of the new chapels of ease,
supported by voluntary effort, which were
springing up in populous parts of the
country, and the ministers of which, not
being parish ministers, could not sit in
Church courts. The Chapel Act, passed

in the same year, put such ministers on an
equality with the rest, and thereby greatly
increased the anti-Moderate element in
future Assemblies.

The Ten Years' Conflict

Thus began what is known as the " Ten
Years' Conflict," in which the whole relations of Church and State were brought into
controversy. The matter at issue was not the
legality of patronage, which was admitted,
but the right of the Church to control its
procedure. The exponents both of the new
evangelicalism and of the new democracy
protested against the notion of a unitary
state with complete jurisdiction over all
departments of life. The old war-cry of
the " Headship of Christ " was heard again,
and there were wild words spoken ; the
extremists, like the Covenanters, were often
deficient in reverence and humour ; the
right to veto a presentee was described as a

right " purchased by the Redeemer with
His blood " ; and there were evangelical
leaders who seemed to advocate a new papal-
ism. But behind the extravagance a great
and historic principle was at stake, the
self-governing powers of the Church. The
pity was that the policy adopted in the
Veto and Chapel Acts kept the quarrel
inside the narrow domain of law. The
difficulty lay in the confounding of two
different words, " jurisdiction " and " authority." The Church could claim authority
derived from its divine founder, but when
it claimed for its courts " exclusive jurisdiction," the right to declare and enforce law,
it entered the perilous pale of legal subtleties. A problem, which should have been
solved by statesmen, was unhappily left to
the lawyers.

A crop of lawsuits, the Auchterarder case,
the Lethendy case, the Marnoch or Strathbogie case, showed that the Scottish tribunals
were adverse to the Church's claim, and the

House of Lords affirmed their judgment.
Then, too late, recourse was had to the
Government. But neither Melbourne nor
his successor Peel was sympathetic. It was
impossible to make an English statesman
understand the true inwardness of a problem
with such an idiomatically Scottish back-
ground. Moreover, there were two special
difficulties. The evangelical party in the
Scottish Church was a High Church party,
making a bold claim for religious independence ; the same claim was being urged by
the Oxford Tractarians, who were associated
with a revolt against Protestantism, as most
men understood it. The Cabinet was
staunchly Protestant, and undoubtedly in
their eyes the Scottish case was fatally pre-
judiced by its points of resemblance with the
Oxford Movement. Again, the claim of the
Church, with its insistence upon " exclusive
jurisdiction," seemed to many inconsistent
with the whole genius of the common law.
As Lord Cockburn put it :

"A claim of jurisdiction by the Church, though only to spiritual effects, altogether exclusive of civil control, is so repugnant to modern British notions, that, after the Court decided it to be ill-founded, it is not wonderful that any Government should recoil from attempting to legalise it, even if it could be supposed that any Parliament could have been got to sanction such a measure. . . . It is plain to me that the Church of Scotland had the jurisdiction, and that its practical exercise, as proved by immemorial experience, was quite safe. But, the decision being otherwise, I do not see how any Government, relishing the decision, could do anything but adopt the law delivered by the Court. Its error lay in relishing it." [1]

The Disruption

For the reform party there could be no going back. In 1842, at the "last Assembly of the united Church of Scotland," a resolution condemning patronage was moved by William Cunningham, supported by

[1] *Journal*, ii. 35.

Chalmers, and carried by a large majority. That Assembly also adopted what became famous as the " Claim of Right," which laid down as the basis of the national Church the sole Headship of Christ, and the government of the Church in the hands of office-bearers distinct from the civil magistrates. The Cabinet received these declarations with apathy and refused to act.   Disruption was now probable ; the defeat in March 1843 of Mr. Fox Maule's motion to appoint a committee to inquire into the whole question made it certain.[1]   On the 18th of May the Assembly met in St. Andrew's Church in Edinburgh, a dramatic scene which has been often described.   The Moderator, Dr. David Welsh, read a solemn protest, and then moved to the door, followed by Chalmers and Candlish and Cunningham

[1] The Scottish members voted for the motion in a proportion of two to one, and the defeat was due to English votes. History repeated itself two years ago when the Revised Prayer-book was rejected by Scottish and Irish votes.

and a host of ministers and elders. Through an alley in a vast multitude they marched down the slopes which look upon the Firth to Tanfield Hall in Canonmills, where Chalmers was chosen Moderator by acclamation, and, after the singing of " Durie's Psalm," [1] the first Assembly was constituted of the Free Church of Scotland.

To Gladstone, the High Churchman, the Disruption seemed a " noble and heart-stirring spectacle." " Away," he cried, " with the senile doctrine that religion cannot live but by the aid of parliaments ! " The cool sagacity of Lord Cockburn pronounced it " the most honourable fact for Scotland that its whole history supplies." Such praise was amply deserved. That four hundred and seventy-four ministers should surrender a certain livelihood for a matter of conscience was a vindication of the essential nobility of human nature. Moreover, this matter of conscience

[1] The 124th in the second Scottish metrical version.

was no mere pedantry, but a profound principle of Scottish religious life. But of the majority who remained behind not all were over-careful of the " loaves and fishes," not all were formalists and reactionaries and obscurantists. There were young men like Norman Macleod, who were afraid—and not without reason—of a new high-flying Presbyterian priestcraft, for a kind of sacerdotalism has always been a peril in the Scottish Church. And many, whose sympathies were with those who broke away, were restrained by the honest belief that the true way of reform does not lie through separation, that a schism once it has taken place is hard to bridge, and that by preserving the historic continuity of an institution there is a hope of its reconstruction which departs if it be split asunder. To such, as to the loyalists in the American Revolution, history has been perhaps somewhat less than just.

The new Free Church must remain to all

time a model of bold and provident organisation. This greatest of Scottish secessions
was a masterpiece of constructive genius.
From the start it undertook all the duties of
a national communion. In its first year it
built five hundred churches ; it founded and
carried on schools and religious ordinances
in every part of the land ; it established its
own colleges, and it supported its own
ministry. It collected money at the rate
of a thousand pounds a day, and thereby
taught Scotsmen a new conception of liber-
ality. Since every overseas missionary but
one had joined it, it carried on its shoulders
the whole missionary burden of the Church
it had left. It had as its leaders the ablest
theologians and the most popular preachers
in Scotland, and it had among its rank and
file the flower of her youth. In such a
situation it was small wonder that the new
Church carried its head high and was not
altogether free from spiritual and intellectual
pride. Lord Cockburn thought that the

splendour of their new position had cured
all the old defects of the anti-Moderates—
" except," he adds dryly, " fanaticism, which
it will probably increase."

" We quit," said Chalmers in a famous
passage, " a vitiated Establishment, but
would rejoice in returning to a pure one.
To express it otherwise, we are the advocates
for a national recognition, and a national
support of religion, and we are not volun-
taries." But though the great majority
shared Chalmers's view on this point, it is
clear that it was not an obligatory article of
belief. Soon after the Disruption the Free
Church had to devise a formula which
should embody its binding principle, and
in that formula establishment was not included. The binding principle was " the
freedom and spirituality of the Church of
Christ and her subjection to Him as her only
Head, and His Word as her only standard."
The form which Chalmers's doctrine came
presently to take was a belief in a national

recognition of religion, an insistence upon the general duty of nations and their rulers to protect the welfare of the Church and the interests of Christianity. It may be best expressed, perhaps, in Cromwell's words : " If any whosoever think the interests of Christians and the interests of the nation inconsistent or two different things, I wish my soul may never enter into their secret." The Free Church did not repudiate an establishment, provided it was combined with complete spiritual independence, but its cardinal principle was the second, and it soon inclined to grow apathetic about the first. It claimed to be the continuing Church of Scotland, the direct heir of the Reformation, the true repository of the traditions of Knox and Melville and Henderson, and such credentials were not made more splendid by any nod of assent from the State.

F

The Abolition of Patronage

Chalmers died and new men appeared, men without his conservatism and deep historic sense, and sometimes without his charity. The new Church advanced from strength to strength, its missionary enterprise brought it the admiration of the world, and soon its scholarship was not less famous than its evangelical zeal. It would have been strange if in such circumstances it had not developed a certain proud exclusiveness. Not all his successors could have said truly with Chalmers, " Who cares about the Free Church compared with the Christian good of the people of Scotland ? . . . Be assured that the moral and religious well-being of the population is of infinitely higher importance than the advancement of any sect." Toleration was not a common mood. Its battles, internal and external, were stubbornly and bitterly fought.

Meantime the Church of Scotland, dazed

for some years by the shock of the Disruption, was slowly putting its house in order. Younger men were arising in its ranks —Norman Macleod, Tulloch and Caird, Charteris and Flint and Story, who had none of the old Moderate obscurantism, and who as preachers, thinkers and ecclesiastical statesmen could compare with the best in any communion. The first duties were to get rid of compromising lumber and to awaken the Church to its proper task. Robertson of Ellon carried out a large scheme of Church extension and endowment, and the duties of education, and of home and foreign missions, were undertaken in a new spirit. In 1852 ecclesiastical tests were abolished in the universities except for theological chairs, and finally, in 1874, after many futile attempts, patronage disappeared.

No doubt there were blunders in tactics. Considering all that had gone before, it would have been well if the Church of Scot-

land had taken the Free Church into its
confidence and carried it with it in the
various stages for the abolition of what had
been the original rock of stumbling. Many
churchmen believed — Norman Macleod
among them—that the disappearance of
patronage would open the road to re-union.
But the Free Church had travelled far since
1843. Towards the removal of the handi-
caps of the sister Church it showed itself
either apathetic or hostile, so that Mr. Arthur
Balfour was compelled to ask in the House
of Commons whether one religious sect could
have a vested interest in the abuses of another. It held, not unnaturally, that what
had driven it into the wilderness should not
be removed without some confession of past
error, or even restitution. It feared that the
now liberated Church of Scotland might
draw to itself seceders from its ranks who
had forgotten, or had never understood,
that patronage was the occasion rather than
the cause of the breach of 1843.

An inevitable outcome was a demand for disestablishment. Resolutions in its favour were carried by large majorities in the Free Church Assembly and the United Presbyterian Synod in 1874. During the next six years the agitation grew, and with the return of Mr. Gladstone to power in 1880 it became a matter of party politics. The Liberal Prime Minister was never more than half-hearted on the question, and the emergence of Irish Home Rule as the main topic of political controversy, and the consequent schism in the Liberal party, put it beyond the sphere of the practicable.

The best of the Free Church leaders advocated disestablishment because they believed that it was the only basis for an ultimate Presbyterian unity in Scotland. But others—as was shown by the opposition to the Bill introduced by Mr. Finlay (afterwards Lord Chancellor of England) to declare the exclusive right of the Church of Scotland to regulate all matters

spiritual by its own courts " not subject
to interdict, reduction, suspension or any
matter of review by any court of civil
jurisdiction "—were influenced by the less
worthy fear of losing, through the abolition
of patronage, members to the other Church.
To the historian it may well appear
that for one communion to enlist the help
of a political party, temporarily in power, in
order to enforce something which another
communion vehemently dislikes was the
extreme of Erastianism, if that word have
any meaning. It was fortunate that the
movement failed, but it may be that the
raising of the question had its own value, for
it beaconed one perilous path, and pre-
vented the minds of those who followed
after unity from straying into fruitless fields.

During those years influences were at work
in Scotland to broaden the dogmatic basis of
faith and to enrich the traditional worship.
There were many who in cult desired to
return to the way of the first Reformers and

to get rid of the alien Puritan belief that
ugliness was indispensable for godliness. In
matters of creed the Free Church was the
pioneer. The tragic issue of the Robertson
Smith case did more to liberalise its theology
than if the great heresiarch had remained in
its fold. It burst for good and all the bonds
of a blind Scripture literalism, and his historical standpoint, in no way inconsistent
with faith, became the creed of all thinking
men. " In the Bible alone I find God drawing near to man in Christ Jesus and declaring
to us in Him His Will for our salvation, and
this record I know to be true by the witness
of His Spirit in my heart, whereby I am
assured that none other than God Himself
is able to speak such words to my soul." In
the Church of Scotland, too, men like John
Caird were linking religion with an idealist
conception of the world, and insisting that
spiritual truths stood in need of constant
re-statement, since creeds and theories are
transient things, and no single one can be

taken as the final and infallible interpretation of God's mind to man. The Church in Scotland, under the challenge of a new environment, was following the inexorable biological law and modifying its structure.

The United Free Church

Meantime, among the non-established Churches, there had been during the century a steady drawing together. The wise course was followed whereby those closest to each other united, and thereby formed a potent centre to attract further adhesions. In 1847, the year of Chalmers' death, in Tanfield Hall, the scene of the Disruption, a new Church was born—the United Presbyterian, formed by the union of the Secession and Relief bodies—a Church at once orthodox and liberal, which was destined to play a great part in the religious life of Scotland. In 1852 the majority of the Original Seceders were received into the Free Church, and in

1876 the majority of the Reformed Presbyterians. Just as in the Free Church some form of establishment was generally accepted as desirable, but was not made a cardinal principle, so among the United Presbyterians what was known as " voluntaryism," while not an obligatory tenet, was the view of the majority.

Voluntaryism meant an aversion not only to State control, but to any kind of State connection. It was not the extreme atomism of Independency, for it contemplated an organised Church. On the negative side it was inclined to the view that a civil government had no concern with religion ; on the positive side it laid down the duty of congregations to support the preaching of the Word by free-will gifts. This positive side alone was included in the standards of the Church ; the negative side was left to the taste of individual members. It may fairly be said that the United Presbyterian Church had not in its articles any

renunciation of an establishment, so long as
spiritual autonomy and religious equality
were safeguarded, or even of endowment,
provided the duty of voluntary giving was
not forgotten.   And in men like John Cairns
there was a burning vision of religious peace
in Scotland—nay, more, of

> " a Church which, while separately organised
> in different countries, shall be one in basis
> and spirit, taking the Reformed Faith as its
> creed, simplicity as its guide in worship, and
> the Bible as its supreme standard, but which
> both in formation and administration must be
> independent and free from control by civil
> powers." [1]

Clearly no barrier of doctrine or practice
stood between the Free Church and the
United Presbyterian Church if establishment was not a cardinal tenet of the one or
voluntaryism of the other.   But this natural
union was long delayed.   From 1863 onward there was a second Ten Years' Conflict

[1] MacEwen, *Life of Cairns*, 301.

within the Free Church on the matter, but
the efforts of the majority were thwarted by
the " Constitutional " party under Begg, and
they relinquished their campaign in fear of
a threatened schism. " Disruption pride '
was still too strong a thing. A tribute is due
from the chronicler to the dignity and
wisdom of the United Presbyterian leaders
during this difficult time.

The movement was resumed in 1896, by
which date both Churches had by means
of declaratory acts broadened the basis of
their articles of faith. This is not the place
to tell the tale of the different stages in the
advance to union, in which Dr. Rainy was
the leader, as he had been the colleague of
Candlish and Buchanan in the abortive
attempt a quarter of a century before. By
1900 all difficulties had been surmounted,
and on the 30th day of October of that year
the Union was formally consummated. The
achievement formed a happy precedent, for
in the new United Free Church neither of

the constituent bodies surrendered anything : things on which they had formerly differed remained open questions ; it was union without uniformity ; the points of contact were the fundamentals.

The Church Case

A section of the more conservative party in the Free Church, mostly living in the Highlands, refused to enter the Union, and constituted themselves the Free Church of Scotland. What followed will be long remembered. They brought an action at law to have themselves declared the historic Free Church and therefore the owners of the Church's property, which was held on trust for the principles of that Church's constitution—principles, they alleged, violated by the Union. They were unsuccessful in the Scottish courts, but in August 1904 the House of Lords on appeal, by a majority of three, gave judgment in their favour. It is probable that future ages will regard the verdict as at least dubious, and look to the dissenting judgments, like Lord Lindley's, for sounder law and sounder history.

But the supreme court of the land had decided, and its judgment must be accepted. Dr. Rainy, now within sight of eighty, faced the crisis in the spirit of Chalmers, and in his third Moderatorship steered his Church through the storm. Money was collected for immediate needs, as in the days of the Disruption ; there were few words spoken of bitterness or complaint ; the help of the State was called in to redress an impossible situation : a Royal Commission divided the property in accordance with the needs and capacities of the two parties, and an Act of Parliament made this apportionment law. A clause in that Act gave the Church of Scotland the right to revise its formula of subscription on the lines of the declaratory acts of the other Churches. In the General Assembly of 1905 the United Free Church

in a solemn declaration reasserted its claim
to spiritual liberty, on lines similar to the
resolution of the Assembly in 1838.

The judgment of the House of Lords was
the proximate cause of Scottish Church
Union.   Already the main obstacles had
gone.   The Covenants, with all their dangerous implications, were now things of only
antiquarian interest.   The Churches had
long withdrawn themselves inside their
spiritual domain and abandoned all theocratic pretensions.   The antique literalism
with which the Bible had been interpreted
was discarded, and their theology had been
at once broadened and vivified.   Patronage
with all its ugly concomitants had disappeared.   Spiritual liberty, which involved
liberty to change within certain limits, had
become everywhere an accepted article of
faith.   There was a juster distinction made
between fundamentals and " circumstantials," between essential tenets and open
questions ; and unity was conceived of as

possible without a drab uniformity. This
general consensus had come about in the
right way, since old dogmas had not been
formally renounced but had faded out of
the intellectual air. A thousand matters of
ancient dispute had become simply meaningless. Toleration, moreover, so far from
being regarded as a soul-killing vice, was
seen to be in itself a religious duty.

The events of August 1904 completed this
clearing of the ground. As far back as 1767
Lord Mansfield had laid it down that
voluntary Churches were "established,"
since, being tolerated, they had a place of
security in the commonwealth.[1] The word
was ceasing to have the sinister connotation
which it had possessed since the Disruption.
It was now clear that from a certain kind of
establishment no Church could be free,
since, if it owned property, it was bound by
the terms of endowment, and, if it sought
to change, might find itself compelled to

[1] *Corporation of London* v. *Evans* (H. of L.), Holliday, 225.

choose between impoverishment and liberty. Declarations of independence were not enough ; it must secure the State's co-operation in safeguarding such independence. The State had restored to the United Free Church the patrimony which it had lost through a lesser union ; it might well be asked to assist in opening the way to a greater.

VI

THE GREAT WAR AND AFTER

Twice in the last century the Church of Scotland had made overtures to the Free Church for some form of co-operation which might lead to union, but the time was not ripe for so bold a venture. But after 1904 the atmosphere had changed, and the problem came out of the mists of idealism into the clearer air of the practicable. On the side of the Church of Scotland Archibald Scott and William Mair were the protagonists, and the leaders of the United Free Church, some of whom had been active in the old disestablishment crusade, were not slow to welcome their advances. One thing was plain : the purpose must be union or nothing, for the Churches were too closely akin for mere co-operation. A long step forward was taken in 1909, when there was a general agreement that the whole ground must be examined by unrestricted conference. Meantime two men had emerged, Dr. John White of the Church of Scotland and Dr. Alexander Martin of the United Free Church, who were to lead the movement to a triumphant conclusion ; while a third, Dr. Archibald Henderson, did much to create within the latter Church the atmosphere without which union was impossible.

It is important to remember the magnitude of the task which confronted the negotiators. The field had indeed been largely cleared, but, when they began their work in 1909, the difficulties still seemed

almost insuperable.   One Church had been
formally pledged by annual resolutions for
nearly half a century to disestablishment
and disendowment as a policy not only of
expediency but of justice, while the other
clung to the historic association with the
State.   It is true that many of the old lines
of division had grown faint, and that the
identity of the two Churches in doctrine,
ritual and government had become clearer.
But this very admitted identity was in itself
an obstacle.   In the words of Lord Sands :

> " The differences which to a stranger seem
> most obscure are often the most difficult to
> reconcile.   When two denominations are separ-
> ated by some difference clear and palpable,
> there may be no need to justify separation.
> The cause is obvious.   But when the difference
> is not of this character, it is felt that separation
> needs to be justified in the eyes of the world,
> and this leads to the attachment of immense
> importance to the ground of quarrel and the
> most tenacious and meticulous adherence to the
> one position or the other."

Here it is needless to trace the various steps by which the ground of difference was narrowed and the ground of agreement enlarged. The memorandum published by Lord Sands in 1912, a document which may well be called epoch-making, simplified the issue by making it clear that freedom from State control was the only possible basis of union, and that such freedom was compatible with all that the Church of Scotland valued in its relations to the State. The next step lay with the Church of Scotland, which had the task of preparing a new series of articles to declare the constitution which it regarded as its charter. It was a delicate task, and was not accomplished without controversy, but in the end it was patent that there was nothing in the creed now defined by the Church of Scotland as its basis which differed in fundamentals from that of the sister Church.

Then in August 1914 came the Great War, which proved to be the final reconciler.

Co-operation there had to be, under the stress of urgent needs both in Scotland and in the field. Ministers of both communions served—after the fine Scottish fashion—not only as chaplains but as combatants, and as platoon and company commanders shed the foibles of clericalism and reached a new understanding of the ordinary man. The social duties of the Church, too often forgotten in ecclesiastical quarrels, were burned in upon such minds. The consequence was that, after the Armistice, it was found that the whole question had undergone a chemical change. The problems of reconstruction were so vast that the Church of Christ could not face them unless it possessed a united front and a unified command.

Dr. Archibald Henderson had already pointed out in 1911 the desperate needs of the new Scotland. Her population had doubled since 1843, and the two Churches did not number among their members and adherents one-half of that population. The distribution

of churches was faulty, and the denomina-
tional rivalry meant a grievous waste of
money and power. The two Churches between them had two hundred congregations
with less than fifty members, and nearly five
hundred with less than a hundred each.
Moreover the War, with its urgent realities,
had cast many old controversial matters still
further back into the antiquarian mists.
Lastly, the whole conception of the State had
changed. Whig individualism had given
place to a deeper and more organic conception of the part of the State in the communal
life. That a Church should have some kind
of relation with the civil Government no
longer seemed a dereliction of Christian
duty.

The new draft articles of the Church of
Scotland, which were in substance akin to
the old " Claim of Right," were nine in
number. The first defined the faith of the
Church as Trinitarian, Evangelical and
Protestant, a sufficiently wide charter, and

power was given to the Church to interpret the terms. The fourth, dealing with spiritual freedom, asserted in the most emphatic terms the separate and independent government and jurisdiction of the Church, and claimed the right and power to legislate, the crucial test of autonomy. The third and sixth insisted in carefully chosen words on the national recognition of religion, not as a new principle but as part of the Church's historic identity. One passage is memorable :

" This Church acknowledges the divine appointment and authority of the civil magistrate within his own sphere, and maintains its historic testimony to the duty of the nation acting in its corporate capacity to render homage to God, to acknowledge the Lord Jesus Christ as the King over the nations, to obey His laws, to reverence His ordinances, to honour His Church, and to promote in all appropriate ways the Kingdom of God. The Church and the State owe mutual duties to each other, and acting within their separate spheres may signally promote each other's welfare. The Church and the State have the right to determine each for itself all questions concerning the extent or the continuance of their mutual relations in the discharge of their duties and the obligations arising therefrom." [1]

It is a far cry from such words to the judgment of Lord President Hope, in the first Auchterarder case, that Parliament was " the temporal head of the Church, from whose acts, and from whose acts alone, it exists as a national Church, and from whom alone it derives all its powers."

The new articles were put in the form of a Bill which passed both Houses of Parliament without a division in the summer of 1921. The Act was not to come into operation till the articles had been adopted by a majority of the presbyteries of the Church of Scotland—which was accomplished by

[1] It re-echoes in parts similar declarations made in earlier times, *e.g.* the Heads of Agreement drawn up between the Free and United Presbyterian Churches in 1869, and even the Basis of Union between Burghers and Anti-Burghers in 1820.

1926. The next problem was the endowments. A commission was appointed to examine the difficult question of the teinds, ancient property rights which it was desirable to change from the position of a fluctuating annual charge to a capital sum, which could be handed over to the Church's keeping. After much negotiation an arrangement was arrived at which became the law of the land in 1925. The Church lost in the transaction nearly one-sixth of its former revenues from this source, but won complete freedom in dealing with what remained.

The Union

The Church of Scotland was now, as to creed, status and property, on the same basis as the sister Church. There remained the slow task of securing that final ratification of union from below, from presbyteries and congregations, which is an essential part of Presbyterian democracy. This task presented no difficulty in the Church of Scotland, but in the United Free Church, where there was an appreciable dissenting minority, and where the subordinate organism was more highly integrated, it required time and a patient diplomacy. In 1926 new committees were appointed in both Churches to conduct the actual negotiations, the leaders being Dr. John White and Lord Sands for the one Church, and Principal Martin and Dr. Drummond for the other. Within a year a provisional agreement was reached on a " Basis and Plan of Union," which during the next two years was carefully examined by the lower Church courts. Counsel's opinion was taken on the question as to whether, in a union with the Church of Scotland on the proposed basis, the property of the United Free Church could without breach of trust be transferred to the United Church. The present Lord Macmillan held that it could, since the Churches differed neither in creed nor ecclesiastical polity, but he advised, in order to make assurance sure, that the United Free Church should, under the terms of its constitution, expressly declare that the two Churches were at one in constitution and principle.

In the Assemblies of 1928 it was evident that the opposition, never formidable, was rapidly shrinking. The Basis of Union was sent down finally under the Barrier Act to the presbyteries, kirk-sessions and congregations being also consulted. In the Church of Scotland every presbytery voted in its favour—seventy-two out of the eighty-four unanimously. In the United Free Church all the sixty-three home presbyteries approved, and there was only a small minority of dissentients among the congregations and sessions. So at long last, in May 1929, when a royal prince acted for the first time as Lord High Commissioner, the Union was ratified by the two Assemblies. In the following October, with the Duke of York again representing the King, the first Union Assembly took place, as described in the succeeding chapter. A small minority constituted a dissenting remnant. It would not have been Scotland without such a protest.

The Church thus reunited is a new type among Christian communions, and it is right to remind ourselves of its conspicuous privileges. For the first time in history we have a Church which is acknowledged by the law of the land to be wholly free : free in its government and jurisdiction, free in its faith, having power to interpret its creeds and to alter them within the wide limits of trinitarian Protestantism, free in its use of its temporalities. And at the same time it is a historic Church, with no gap in its continuity from the first Reformers, cherishing its ancient documents of title, recognised by the State as the national representative of the faith of the Scottish people—the Church of Scotland, and not merely a

Church in Scotland. The words " established " and " dis-established " have no
longer any but an historical meaning. The
Church is that far greater thing, a national
Church, as it was in 1560 at its beginnings.

Retrospect

Looking back on the long story, it may
well seem that no stage was without its
beneficent purpose. Each schism, each controversy had its place in a great plan, for
each emphasised a facet of the truth which
was in danger of neglect. Men who seceded
on one point gravely over-emphasised that
point, but their secession and their over-
emphasis secured for whatever it contained
of substance a place in the national testimony. The extravagance of the seven-
teenth-century theocrats made it certain
that no Church would ever command the
assent of the Scottish people which was in
spiritual bondage to the civil power, and

when this article seemed in peril the eighteenth-century seceders rose to affirm it. The "voluntary" movement taught the economic side of autonomy and the importance of religious equality ; those who clung to the establishment preserved the belief in a national recognition of religion. The strength of the nineteenth-century free communions gave a chance both for the liberalisation of confessions and for a larger view of the social duties of the Christian faith.

Slowly, painfully, the Church rid itself of certain sinister heritages ; it shed the mediaevalism which made it a rival of the State ; it abandoned its narrow Scriptural literalism ; it learned that toleration was not a pagan vice but a Christian virtue, and that the path to unity did not lie through a bleak uniformity. But all these lessons would have been vain had not a vision of the peace and felicity of a united Jerusalem survived among good men in each generation, even when their conscience demanded a further disruption. The very vigour of their scruples and their honest resolution to be loyal to what they held to be truth made it certain that unity if attained would be no shallow, unfeatured thing, but a living organism in which all that was of value in old differences would be transmuted and reconciled.

> " Why else was the pause prolonged but that
> singing might issue thence ?
> Why rushed the discords in but that har-
> mony should be prized ? "

From the standpoint of the goal attained we can retrace the road and see how all the pilgrims, even in their deviations, contributed something to its attainment. One lightened the baggage and was cast out, but in time what he had rejected was left behind by all. Another took a course of his own in sterile country, but his followers stumbled upon Pisgah-views and returned to the main march with a new vision. Others stuck by the path which ordinary folk could travel, and formed a rallying point to unite the stragglers.

These men, moving down through the ages, are many of them great figures, attaining often to heroic stature, men who had the making of their country in their hands, for the history of Scotland is largely the history of her Church. Some are still in our memories—Rainy and Caird and Story, with faces cast in a mould of antique dignity. Behind them we see Norman Macleod with his kindly sagacity and Highland fire, and the noble head of Cunningham, and Candlish's short, gnarled figure, and John Cairns' rugged face, and Chalmers with the brow of the mathematician and the eyes of the visionary. . . . Further back are the perukes of the eighteenth century—the bland precision of Blair ; the black mittens of Webster ; Carlyle of Inveresk, handsome as a pagan god ; the great chin and the bright, vivacious eyes of Principal Robertson ; the

Erskines, too, with their high foreheads and lips pursed as if in an eternal protest, and Boston of Ettrick, pale with fasting and study, and William Carstares, heavy-wigged, heavy-browed, his fingers crooked from the torture-chamber. . . . Beyond them are the men of the heather, lean, wild folk, short-lived for the most part and tragically fated, with voices shrill from hillside preaching and eyes pale like a seaman's from hilltop watches. . . . Then come the skull-caps and bands of the divines who saw their Church on the pinnacle of its temporal power—the " fair little man," half jurist, half dreamer, who was Samuel Rutherford, and Alexander Henderson, his skin yellow with ague and his eyes hollow with unsleeping thought, a statesman born in an ill season for statesman-ship. . . . Now we are among the flat caps of the Reformers, chief of them Knox with his hawk's nose and hawk's eye and patri-arch's beard, the man who had the passion-ate momentum of some great portent of nature. . . . Then the mists descend, and we see only dim figures in proud hieratic robes, and sometimes under the robes a gleam of steel, for they were often of the church militant, and served in the field as well as at the altar. . . . But in the far distance the air clears, and against a Hebridean sky we can discern him who was called the Dove and was both priest and prince, and who on another isle, like John on Patmos, had visions of a peace among men which " has its birth in mortal love, but its evening home where are the dews of immortality."

THE   UNION   ASSEMBLY

CHAPTER II

THE UNION ASSEMBLY

OF General Assembly weather in May, Russell of *The Scotsman* was wont to write that " as usual the east wind keeps covenant with the Fathers and Brethren." For the Re-Union Assembly of October 1929, it was the west wind, in rapid gusts and at times a gale, which for the most part blew through a snell, grey air, and scoured the streets and roofs with rain, yet now and then allowed a burst of sunshine. And Edinburgh was herself in other ways. She greeted the Re-Union of the Scottish Churches with the eager crowds which in all other crises of the nation's history have filled her streets and gazed from the windows of her high " lands." As is her hospitable wont, she put at the disposal of the Assembly both her Old and her New Town. And all her distant prospects of the country were clear, of which, as becomes the Capital, her eyes command a wider range than do those of any other Scottish city. North, south, east and west the approaches were visible, by which over land and sea the representatives of the Scottish people were hastening to take part in the greatest national demonstration of our time, greater perhaps than any that ever happened. As we beheld the city and her approaches we remembered that, though often the scene of strife, secession and disruption both in State and Church during our " stormy and gallant history," [1] she had also proved more than once the source of law and order in Scotland and the stage of Church Union. She is " the heart of Scotland, and each throb that she gives is felt from the edge of Solway to Duncansbayhead." [2]   Her bells were ringing, but above

[1] Principal Story.
[2] Walter Scott : *The Abbot.*

them to our hearts rang her sacred motto, *Nisi Dominus Frustra* ; for as we trod the way to St. Giles we felt that except the Lord had been with us, through the long and complex negotiations of these last twenty years, we had never reached the sacred consummation of our efforts.

THE LAST SEPARATE ASSEMBLIES

On 24th May 1929, the two General Assemblies, " finding that the Overtures anent the Basis of Union and the Plan of Union have obtained under the Barrier Act the requisite approbation of the Presbyteries " of their respective Churches, had " resolved upon an incorporating Union with each other." This the Church of Scotland Assembly did after approving of the report of their Committee, that by such a Union " the differences which for generations have been the cause of separation will have been reconciled without any breach of continuity, and the great body of Scottish Presbyterians will have been gathered into one national and historic Church without any surrender of principle or sacrifice of cherished traditions." The United Free Church Assembly reached their resolution having " determined and declared that after the changes effected in the constitution and relation to the State of the Church of Scotland by the Acts of 1921 and 1925," as also in view of other matters, " there is in the relation of the Church of Scotland to the State nothing which is inconsistent with the constitution of the United Free Church of Scotland and the principles thereof."

On Tuesday, 1st October, the two General Assemblies, or, to use their ancient title, the Convocations, of the Church of Scotland, met apart for business for the last time. They had now only to approve of the reports and recommendations of their respective Committees in completion of the Plan of

Union, and then adjourn to unite on the following day. While a natural sympathy was expressed by each House with the personal ties and sacred associations of their separate careers, which must be left behind, in both there was the calm and joyful note of a clear and honest confidence in the step they were about to take and in the future to which it was leading.

The General Assembly of the Church of Scotland, in presence of the Lord High Commissioner, His Grace the Duke of York, and under their Moderator, the Right Reverend Joseph Mitchell, D.D., passed the relevant resolutions unanimously and without discussion. The mover of these, Dr. John White of the Barony, after thanking Mr. J. J. Herdman, W.S., for his long and arduous share in the labours of the Conferring Committee, and the Moderator for the characteristic thoroughness and loyalty with which he had discharged his office, continued : " The hour of action has come. We go forward to-morrow to consummate the Union for which we have so long laboured and prayed. It is to-day, as the last word is spoken, that the solemnity of the course to which we have committed ourselves is so keenly felt. We realise that we are parting with some very sacred associations, very dear for our fathers' sakes and doubly precious from our own experience, but we are giving up nothing which they held dear, we take with us the heritage they left intact. . . . We go forward with full assurance of hope to meet the new horizon to which our God of hope is summoning us." And in seconding the resolutions, Lord Sands, with reminiscences of the era which was closing, said : " I venture to affirm, standing here after these eighty-six years of separation, that our Church has vindicated her position—I do not mean her controversial position, but her position and her claim as a living Church, an evangelical Church, in Scotland, a missionary Church abroad, and a great witness to the principle of the national recognition of religion."

In closing this Diet of the Assembly, the Moderator reviewed his experience of office and added these words : " Everywhere I found, as was to be expected, evidence of activity and enthusiasm in support of the Church's work. It is not a somnolent or a moribund Church that we carry into the Union. It is a Church full of vigour and of zeal, awake to the needs of the time and eager to bear its part in the establishment and the advancement of God's Kingdom. . . . We are going into the Union whole-heartedly and unreservedly, and putting our whole strength into the task which lies before us of claiming Scotland for Christ and making that claim effective. We leave nothing which is of value from the religious point of view. We take with us everything of power to promote the spiritual welfare of the nation. And we are confident that, with the contribution which we bring, with that which is brought by those with whom we are uniting, with the added strength which comes from the combination of our forces, and with the inspiration of the Divine Spirit which is promised and given to those who truly seek the furtherance of God's Kingdom, the re-united Church of Scotland will go from strength to strength, and to the generations that are yet to come, as to those who have been blest to see this day, will prove the greatest power for good that this nation has ever known, to the praise and glory of God's Holy Name."

The other Assembly had still to meet the opposition to Union of a small minority— only some twenty-two out of a member-ship in a House of nearly 1200, and even smaller than the minorities of forty-eight and thirty-nine in the Assemblies of November 1928 and May 1929, but as firm as ever in refusing to enter the re-united Church—and with these the Assembly had to part. Even this sore separation was effected in the peace and Christian temper on both sides which had dignified the discussions between them from first to last. The Assembly agreed (as had been arranged in Committee) to grant the minority under the name of The United Free Church (Continuing) £25,000 " in full settlement of their interests in the general funds and property of the Church " ; and the minority " disclaimed any intention of litigation." In moving the adoption of these and other proposals of the reporting Committee, Dr. R. J. Drummond fitly said : " What they had to be thankful for in that regrettable matter was that they had endeavoured and succeeded in keeping the unity of the spirit in the bond of peace. They parted from their brethren in terms of respect and goodwill." And in seconding, on behalf of the eldership of the Church, Sir William Henderson of Dundee, paid tribute " to the great work which had been done by the Moderator and Dr. Drummond, and those who were commissioned to carry out the delicate details of the settlement in conference with the minority."

In his closing address as Moderator, Dr. Alexander Martin, calling on the Assembly to stand, finely declared : " Let me testify in your name, as in my own, reverently and humbly and with a full heart, ' Hitherto hath the Lord helped us. There has not failed us aught of any good thing which the Lord hath spoken unto the House of Israel ; all has come to pass.' For the future it is a common sorrow that we do not enter upon it with ranks unbroken. But here, too, the record is closed. We can but leave our severance at the feet of the Church's Head. May He pardon and overrule that which in our infirmity we have been unable to avert, and out of it, in His Wisdom, bring forth good for His Name's sake. And for one another as we go our separate ways, as for those whom on the morrow we rejoin, we sum up all our desires in the prayer, ' The

Lord our God be with us as He was with our fathers.' "

THE DAY OF UNION

After a night of wind and rain, the great day of Union, Wednesday, 2nd October 1929, dawned in storm, but, as it proved, with some fair weather ahead and gleams of sunshine for the hour of the Processions to St. Giles. All praise to those who had devoutly planned that, before engaging in the formal process of Union, the two General Assemblies should seek the House of God for His Blessing and offer " a service of thanksgiving and dedication."

For the last time the Assemblies were separately constituted by Prayer and the Word, and punctually at 10.20—the exact moment is historic—they started from the Tolbooth Kirk and the Assembly Hall, the one down the Lawnmarket, the other up the Mound and Bank Street, to meet on

Edinburgh's Historic Mile, where the Lawn-market yields to the High Street and St. Giles stands full in view. The scene is classic in the religious history of our people ; what fitter could there be for such a union of hearts ! The two Moderators clasped hands, and the rest of us, falling in behind them and the Moderator-Designate, marched four abreast in the following order : The Clerks of Assembly and the Procurator, the ex-Moderators headed by the venerable Dr. Laws of Livingstonia, the Principals and Professors of the Divinity Faculties, Lord Sands and the Joint Union Committee, and then the other members of the Two Houses, ministers and elders. We had no military or civic escort, there was no pomp or pageantry, not even ornament, save the dark robes and coloured hoods of the Moderators and ex-Moderators — nothing but a long stream of deep hearts and stead-fast wills reverently passing to the House of the Lord through Edinburgh's historic welcome of streets and windows, crowded with eager, earnest faces.

With what memories those hearts were stirred! It was John Knox's Parish we were treading and to John Knox's Kirk we were bound. The shades of many captains and witnesses for the truth seemed to be with us, from Andrew Melville and Samuel Rutherford to Thomas Chalmers and Norman Macleod, John Cairns and Robert Rainy. Yet chiefly we felt led by the pioneers of Union in our own time —Archibald Scott and Lord Balfour of Burleigh; Archibald Henderson, George Robson and Alexander MacEwen; Cameron Lees, Donald Macleod and Wallace Williamson. As the processions met we caught from the cheering crowds the strains of psalm and paraphrase: " Behold how good a thing it is in unity to dwell," " Now Israel may say, and that truly," " The Lord 's my Shepherd," and " O God of Bethel." Manifestly, the Scottish people were with their Churches.

I

At the west door of St. Giles the procession was met by the minister, the Very Reverend Charles L. Warr, Dean of the Thistle, and his fellow-ministers. The Dean shook hands with the Moderators and greeted them with the words : " Now is the Son of Man glorified. Peace be unto you."

As we waited for the service, our hearts throbbing to the quiet footfalls of that long procession of all classes of the realm, our thoughts went back to Knox's preaching there to the " haill nobilitie and the greatest part of the congregation." But later, when we stood, as, guided by the Moderators, the Moderator-Designate, and the Dean of the Thistle, Their Royal Highnesses the Duke and Duchess of York passed up the aisles to the Royal Pew, our thoughts travelled back still further to the days of King Malcolm and Queen Margaret ; and the gratitude which then held the capital and the country was renewed in our sense of having once again to reign over us " a God-fearing

AT THE DOOR OF ST. GILES

House." Yet in our hearts the chief joy was to behold how religion, so long a disruptive force in Scotland, was now a uniting power. Through all the negotiations between our two Churches it was the predominance of purely spiritual aims and their blessed consequences of mutual understanding and charity, which had overcome the age-long estrangements and prejudices, and now at last achieved this Union in honest peace and confidence in each other, for which we were met to thank our God.

The service—and none more stirring and impressive was ever held even in St. Giles— was wholly devotional : Prayers, Praises and Readings of the Word, led successively by the two Moderators and their Chaplains. To its affianced tune of "St. Paul" we sang the Assembly Psalm, the Hundred-and-Twenty-Second, " I joyed when to the House of God, Go up they said to me. . . . Pray that Jerusalem may have Peace and Felicity." Dr. Mitchell then said, " Dearly

Beloved Brethren, We are gathered here to invoke the blessing of Almighty God on these branches of His Holy Catholic Church in this our land, and with humble hearts to thank Him for the grace which has brought us to this day. Wherefore let us lift up our souls unto Him in godly fear and childlike trust, giving Him praise for the unity into which we have been led, and dedicating ourselves and all our faithful people, as heirs together of the great salvation, to the faith of His Son, Christ Jesus our Lord, and to the service of His eternal Kingdom." The Hundredth Psalm was sung and Dr. Mitchell led us in a prayer of confession, thanksgiving and dedication, concluding with our Lord's Prayer, in which all joined. Psalm cxlviii. 1-7 was sung to " St. Andrew." The Old Testament Lesson, Isaiah lxi., followed, then the Te Deum, and the New Testament Lesson, Ephesians iv. 1-16 ; we said the Apostles' Creed ; Dr. Martin led us in a prayer of intercession, and the Hymn *Veni*

Creator was sung. Then came the Benediction, followed by the National Anthem.

Thus Presbyterian in its simplicity and in
its use of the Scottish Metrical Psalms, the
service, by the introduction of the Apostles'
Creed, the *Te Deum*, and the *Veni Creator
Spiritus*, testified, as the Kirk of Scotland
has ever testified, to her substantial oneness
with the Catholic Church of believers
throughout the world, the Church of the
Apostles, the Christian Fathers, and all the
Reformed Churches of Europe. And upon
that Catholic note we rose in the last prayer
to the Communion of the Saints above :
" We bless Thee for all who have laboured
for the peace and unity of Thy Church and
by faith have seen this day, and for those
whom we have in remembrance now before
Thee. . . . Compassed about with so great
a cloud of witnesses, may we lay aside every
weight and the sin which doth so easily
beset us, and run with patience the race that
is set before us, looking unto Jesus the Author

and Finisher of our faith. Keep us united to them in fellowship of spirit ; and grant that inspired by their example we may follow in their steps. And vouchsafe unto us at the last that we may be presented with them before the Presence of Thy Glory with exceeding joy." All those high notes of the service rang out again in our Recessional Hymn, " The Church's One Foundation."

Hitherto the proceedings had all taken place in Old Edinburgh. But for the Re-Union Assembly we passed over to the New Town, the Old having no covered space ample enough for the Great Event. Nor was the change without historic fitness. For on the 18th May, 1843, the New Town and its Kirk of St. Andrew had been the scene of the Disruption, and in the New Town for the first time in our history two General Assemblies were constituted, that of the Free Church of Scotland in a roughly adapted storehouse in Canonmills, called

Tanfield Hall, with seats for 3000. Not many hundred yards from both these sites there stands to-day a huge motor garage of steel and concrete, with a glazed roof upon iron pillars and a stone floor, which by the skill of the Scottish artist, Sir D. Y. Cameron, was transformed into a dignified Assembly Hall—draped in soft colours, comfortably floored and seated for 12,000 people ; furnished, too, with voice-multipliers, as its extent demanded. Along part of one of its rectangular sides ran a platform, and behind this a Throne Gallery for the Lord High Commissioner. Long before the opening of proceedings at two o'clock host upon host of people flowed through the many doors to take their numbered seats, the members of the uniting Assemblies in front of the platform and all the rest around them, filling the vast area to its utmost corners, but all without crowding or disorder, so excellent was the plan which was now carried out by a hundred students acting as ushers.

On the platform, besides the two Moderators, the Clerks, the Procurator and other officials, Lord Sands and the ex-Moderators, sat His Majesty's Secretary of State for Scotland, the Judges of the Court of Session in their robes and full-bottomed wigs, with the Lord President and the Lord Justice-Clerk at their head ; the Lord Provosts, Provosts and Magistrates of several of the leading Scottish burghs ; Lord-Lieutenants of Shires and others of the nobility ; Principals of the Universities, Professors and teachers ; prominent members of other professions, including soldiers of high rank ; along with deputies and guests from the Protestant Churches of Europe, America, South Africa, and Australia, conspicuous among whom were the Archbishop of Canterbury and Lord and Lady Davidson of Lambeth. The great concourse rose in silence when the Duke and Duchess of York with their suite entered the Throne Gallery and took their places.

As our eyes passed from the Royal Presence across the brilliant rows of all ranks
and professions on the platform to the still
more wonderful sea of faces which filled the
vast body of the Hall, we were sure that
never before had there been seen in Scotland
so great a national gathering or one so representative of her people as a whole.   Indeed
there was even more than this.   It was " in-
comparably," as the *Glasgow Herald* said,
" the largest, the most cosmopolitan and the
most representative assemblage of Christian
men and women ever brought together for
such a purpose."

To such a House, at two o'clock, Principal
Martin, who had taken the Chair, gave out
Psalm cii. 13-18, " Thou shalt arise, and
mercy yet Thou to Mount Sion shalt extend," which on the solemn notes of " Duke
Street " spread like a tide across the congregation and rose in a glorious volume of
praise from the whole twelve thousand.
The Lesson, from Philippians ii. 1-11, was

read by Dr. Harvey, Senior Clerk of the
United Free Church, and Dr. Martin led us
in prayer. The Clerks laid upon the table
the minutes of their respective Assemblies,
the records of their agreement upon the
Uniting Act, and other documents. Then
Lord Sands — to whom could the duty
have been more deservedly entrusted ?—
moved the decisive Resolution of Union.
In this, after the requisite preamble, devout
acknowledgment of Divine Guidance, and
prayer for the outpouring of The Spirit,
the two General Assemblies " do now, as in
the Presence of God, adopt the Uniting Act,
including the Basis of Union and the accom-
panying Plan of Union, with the Questions
and Formula for use at the Ordination and
Induction of a Minister, and do hereby . . .
Enact and Declare in the Name of the Lord
Jesus Christ, the great Head of the Church,
that these Churches, being historic branches
of the Reformed Church in Scotland, do and
shall henceforth constitute One Church,

and that the name of the United Church shall be The Church of Scotland."

Lord Sands began with a catholic tribute to the early missionaries of the Cross in Scotland, to the Reformers, to " those who in the following century laboured and suffered in their conflict against the domination of the State over the liberties of the Church and the religious convictions of the people," to " the fathers who in later times for conscience' sake forsook their homes and went out into the wilderness, not counting the cost," as equally to " those who undismayed by loss wrought diligently to restore their Church, and yearned and laboured for long years to repair the breach ; but more especially with gratitude and affection to the men who began the work which has to-day been completed, and who have since passed on."

He continued : " We have wrought a great work in our day. All unworthy as were the best among us, it has been given

to us to close one of the rents in the
seamless robe—a small rent it may appear,
if one regards the world as a whole,
but a great gaping rent in Scotland. Towards the close of last century the cleavage was complete. Christian brotherhood,
always hampered, was sometimes shamed.
Rivalry and jealousy we could not escape.
After a time, indeed, Union began to seem
not impossible. But that it should be
effected, as it is to-day, without any bitterness, on equal terms, with equal honour to
both Churches, and with equal respect for
the ideals which through long years of
separation both had separately cherished,
would have then appeared an idle dream.
Yet this is the work which under the good
hand of God has been brought to-day to full
fruition. Faith, hope and charity have all
played their part ; and if there was one other
needed virtue not lacking, it was courage,
inspired by a great vision. Not unto us but
to His Name be the praise ! . . . Three

great tasks lie before the United Church—
to carry the gospel into the homes of the
people in every corner of the land by in-
tensive territorial work ; to gain and keep a
hold upon the rising generation and train
them in the love and fear of God ; to carry
the Royal Banner to the nations in the far-
flung mission-fields of the world. . . . Scotland for Christ !   Christ to the world ! "

Such in summary was a noble speech,
worthily seconded by Dr. R. J. Drummond, who, speaking for the United Free
Church, traced the streams, Secession, Relief, Burgher and Anti-Burgher, Reformed
Presbyterian, Free Church and United
Presbyterian, of which that Church was the
Union.   These bodies withdrew not from the
Church of Scotland but from its judicatories,
and now, by its own decisive action, that
Church has secured legislation by which
what was offensive has been removed.   Why
then should the two Churches not unite?   To
remain separate would be unmeaning and

to sin against the light.   From the few who have left us we part with sincere regret and respect for their convictions, but there is no shadow of a doubt what the mind of the Church is.   It says " Unite," and the voice of all Scotland, nay, of evangelical Christendom, re-echoes the word. . . . " Into the re-united Church of Scotland from which we all sprang we each bring our various gifts, cherished convictions, traditions and sacred memories, and these from this day become our common heritage.   All are ours, and with humility we say, ' We are Christ's and Christ is God's.'   We enter this Union in obedience to conscience, to the call of duty and under the guidance of the Holy Spirit in answer to prayer.   Our missionaries in heathen lands, and the new communities springing up all over our own, alike call us to join our forces.   When our forefathers went out it was with the prayer that the day might come when the breach would be healed, and do we not recognise that here indeed is the answer to their prayers and to ours ? "

The great House rose to the Motion as one man, the members holding up their right hands.

Principal Martin then said : " In the presence of Jesus Christ, the King and Head of the Church, I declare the Act of Union to have been finally adopted, and that the Church of Scotland and the United Free Church of Scotland, each in fidelity to its great heritage, are now become One Church in Christ Jesus, under the designation of The Church of Scotland."

He then left the Chair and stood to the right of it, while Dr. Joseph Mitchell stood on the other side.

Dr. Mitchell : " In the faith of Jesus Christ, our Divine King and Head, I do now in the name of The Church of Scotland seal and ratify the Union betwixt us made, in token whereof I offer you the right hand of fellowship."

Principal Martin : " In the faith of Jesus Christ, our Divine King and Head, I do now in the name of The United Free Church of Scotland seal and ratify the Union betwixt us made, in token whereof I offer you the right hand of fellowship."

They clasped hands and Dr. Mitchell said : " And here in the Presence of God Most High we pledge ourselves together in solemn covenant " ; and Principal Martin responded : " And in the Name of the Father, and of the Son, and of the Holy Spirit we invoke the Divine Blessing on our Act."

We sang Psalm lxxii. 18, 19, and the Uniting Act was signed by the Moderators and the Clerks of the two Assemblies. The Great Union was completed. The prayers, the tears of centuries, were answered, and we could not but feel that our fathers and fore-fathers were rejoicing with us.

Dr. Joseph Mitchell then took the Chair and with prayer constituted the first General

Assembly of the Church of Scotland Re-united ; the Clerks submitted the rolls of the two uniting Houses, which were adopted as the Roll of the General Assembly of the Church of Scotland ; and the Assembly pro-ceeded to elect a Moderator.

ELECTION OF A MODERATOR

Principal Martin : " Fathers and Breth-ren, the first duty of the Assembly now constituted is to appoint one of its number to the Moderatorial Chair. The office is almost as old as the Reformation. It was in 1563 that it was first ' proposed be the haill Assemblie that ane Moderator should be appointed for avoiding confusion in reasoning and that every brother should speak in his ain roume ' (or turn), and (as added later) ' with modestie.' I cannot believe that this duty on this occasion will present much difficulty ; in the intervening centuries it has not infrequently been other-

K

wise. Our Assembly is a notable one. It will rank in history with the first of all in the Magdalen Chapel of this city in December, 1560, the Second Reformation Assembly of 1638, that of the Revolution Settlement, 1690, and that of 1843. For such an Assembly a Moderator is required of corresponding stature and power. We have him in the brother whom it is my privilege to name. For its first Moderator our Church chose ' The Superintendent of the West,' and we gladly follow the precedent now. Dr. White's diocese, however, is wider even than the West. He is a possession of the whole Church, enjoying not least the confidence and esteem of that section to which he does not himself belong. Of his heroic service to the cause of Union it would be superfluous to speak ; and we are all one in our expectation of the guidance and inspiration which, by God's blessing, he will contribute in the days to come. No one is more deserving of honour at the Church's hands ; by none could we be represented more worthily. Fathers and Brethren, I submit to your suffrages for election as Moderator of the first General Assembly of the re-united Church of Scotland the name of our able, devoted and trusted brother, Dr. John White."

This motion, seconded by Mr. William Whitelaw, LL.D., Elder, Hatton, was unanimously adopted. The Moderator was escorted to the Chair by the ex-Moderators and Senior Clerks of Assembly, welcomed by Dr. Mitchell, assured of the confidence and support of all his brethren ; and the Moderator's ring was put upon his finger.

The House upstanding, Dr. J. T. Cox, one of the Senior Clerks, then read the King's Commission to His Royal Highness Prince Albert Frederick Arthur George, Duke of York, K.G., K.T., K.C.M.G., G.C.V.O., appointing him to represent His Royal Person in this Assembly, and the Commission, received with all honour and respect, was ordered to be recorded. Then followed His Majesty's Letter to the General Assembly, read by the other Senior Clerk, Dr. Harvey.

THE KING'S LETTER

" Right Reverend and Well Beloved, we greet you well. It was with unfeigned satisfaction that we learned that the Church of Scotland and the United Free Church of Scotland had at the recent sittings of their Assemblies confirmed and ratified the proposals for the Union of the Churches. We appreciate the complexity of the problems which had to be solved and the difficulties which had to be surmounted, and we believe that the guidance of the Almighty has been abundantly given to all those who have laboured to this end.

" We have cause, at this time, to render thanks to the Almighty that by His mercy and grace His hand has spared us to witness the consummation of your efforts, and although it will not be possible for us personally to visit, as we had hoped, this first Assembly of the re-

THE MODERATORS AND THE LORD HIGH
COMMISSIONER

united Church, yet it is a source of deep joy and of gratitude to God that we are able to address you on this memorable occasion, to assure you of our great interest in your festival of Union, and to convey to you our earnest hope and confidence that our beloved Church of Scotland will from henceforth be even more abundantly blessed in her labours for the proclamation of the gospel to the people, and the advancement of the spiritual life of the realm.

" We have thought it fitting that our most dear son Albert, Duke of York, whom we appointed to represent us at the last Assembly of the Church prior to the Union, should again act as our representative at the first Assembly of the united Church. We trust that our choice will commend itself to you, the more so as his reception at your former meetings gave happy evidence of the loyalty to the Throne which has always heartened us by its constancy and fervour.

" We assure you of our unwavering concern for the maintenance of the rights and liberties of the Church of Scotland as happily secured, and with our earnest prayer that now and in the years to come you may be filled with the power of the Spirit and that the grace of God may bless and sanctify your labours, we bid you most heartily farewell.

" Given at our Court of St. James's this eighteenth day of September, 1929, in the twentieth year of our reign.   By His Majesty's Command.

" (Sgd.)   WM. ADAMSON."

The Lord High Commissioner was greeted with loud and hearty cheers as he rose to address the House in the following terms :

" Right Reverend and Right Honourable,— I shall count it one of the happiest and most important events in my life to have been present as His Majesty's representative at this, the first, Assembly of the re-united Church of Scotland.   The occasion is one for deep rejoic- ing amongst all those who have the spiritual welfare of this country at heart, but I must leave it to others better qualified for the task to interpret the emotions which upon this solemn occasion must fill all hearts in this great As- sembly.   It is, however, right that I should convey to you the full assurance of His Majesty's interest in and love for the Church of Scotland, of his great sense of zeal for her service, and of his determination to uphold the cause of Presbyterian Government in Scotland.

" Right Reverend Moderator,—I congratulate you most heartily upon your election as Moderator of this memorable Assembly. By the devotion and the unfailing ability with which you have served the Church and the cause of Union you have not only endeared yourself to all on whose behalf you have laboured, but have most fully earned that high distinction which has at this time been conferred upon you by the unanimous voice of your brethren of both the uniting Churches.

" Right Reverend and Right Honourable,— It is, I know, a disappointment to you that the King was unable, owing to the state of his health, to carry out his intention of visiting this Assembly in person. His Majesty also is most keenly disappointed, and he has asked me to inform you that he had, before his illness, been eagerly contemplating the prospect of a visit to an Assembly which marks such a significant event in the history of his beloved Scottish people.

" I understand that since your meetings in May last, all necessary arrangements have been harmoniously completed for the amalgamation and co-ordination of the many agencies of both Churches. This difficult and exacting labour has been shared by many whom you hold in honour. I have already referred to the part which your Moderator has played in the conduct of the movement, but it is fitting that I should couple with his name that of Principal Martin, whose leadership and guidance have been the counterpart of his own.

" Right Reverend and Right Honourable,— Your deliberations at this time will necessarily be brief, but they will hold the promise for future years of renewed strength in the furtherance of the great aims of the Churches, and now, in the name of His Majesty, I most earnestly commend your work and the fruits of the Union so happily completed to the blessing and guidance of Almighty God."

The Moderator, in reply, said :

" May it please Your Royal Highness : The General Assembly rejoices that the King has commissioned Your Royal Highness to attend on this historic occasion, and to bring his gracious and heartening message. We are

profoundly grateful to Your Royal Highness,
not only for honouring us with your presence
at this memorable Assembly, but most of all
for the deep personal interest Your Royal
Highness has taken in the reunion movement.

" It was the fond hope of his Scottish People
that His Majesty, our beloved King, would
have been sufficiently restored to health to be
here in person, and we are much touched by
His Majesty's expression of disappointment
that, owing to the state of his health, it has been
impossible to visit this Assembly in person.

" Greater than any disappointment which
this Assembly feels is their thankfulness to God
who has heard the prayers of the people for
their beloved Sovereign, and is renewing his
strength.

" We are deeply grateful that our Sovereign
has not only sent a gracious message, whose
terms we shall not readily forget, but that His
Majesty has given that message a personal
touch by transmitting it to this General Assembly by the hands of a son who has already
won our hearts.   The General Assembly gives
Your Royal Highness a loyal and affectionate
welcome ; it is with the utmost pleasure that
we greet also Her Royal Highness the Duchess

of York, who has returned to grace our Assembly.

" May it please your Grace : The General Assembly has heard with feelings of deep satisfaction and with profound respect the terms of His Majesty's gracious message. The General Assembly and the whole Church will be greatly encouraged in its work for the spiritual good of our beloved country by this renewed assurance of His Majesty's interest in and love for the Church of Scotland, and of his determination to uphold the cause of Presbyterian government in Scotland ; of his solicitude for the religious welfare of his Scottish People ; and also of his personal interest in the success which has accompanied our long endeavours to heal the divisions of the Church in Scotland. We are grateful to God Who has led His Church in Scotland into this closer fellowship, and has accomplished for the good of His Church the thing we prayed for, but of ourselves were unable to perform. It will be our earnest prayer and our endeavour that this memorable Assembly may be so guided and ruled in its decisions that all may be for the glory of God, for the furtherance of the gospel, for the deepening of the spirit of Christian unity amongst the

Churches, and for the promotion of the highest welfare of the people of His Majesty's ancient kingdom of Scotland."

The Moderator's Address

Turning to the House, the Moderator then delivered his address. The following is but a summary of the comprehensiveness, the impartiality, the practical wisdom and the spiritual power by which this utterance rose the solemn and historic occasion.

Acknowledging the goodwill of the Assembly to himself, giving thanks to God, Who had brought us to this hour of answered prayer, and calling us to a fresh consecration to His Service, Dr. White honoured the memory of our fellow-builders who led in our reconstruction in 1909 and who, though summoned hence before the copestone was placed, are with us still ; as well as the memory of the pioneers of Union before 1909, and their sacrifices ; adding that while we should make defection from their faith and loyalty, if we regarded any of them as infallible or shut ourselves off from the Divine lessons to our own time, yet those memories must inspire us with the conscience of our own opportunities and responsibilities.

We are joint-heirs of all that our troubled but glorious past transmits ; one in a common profession of faith ; one in the inherent right to interpret that faith and to govern our forms of worship ; one in our respect for God's ordinance of magistracy ; one in our faithfulness to the Presbyterian system, as democratic in principle, free in its operations, loyal to Catholic faith and order ; and one in the purpose to bring our nation to acknowledge the Rule of Christ. Our unity and continuity is no rigid sameness, but is constantly enriched by the contributions of the various branches without surrender of principle or cherished tradition, the Church's duty being to comprehend, not to compromise, and to see that any truth, too lightly regarded hitherto or magnified in isolation, is balanced by compensating truths. And in the front of our testimony we claim part in the Holy Catholic or Universal Church, worshipping God in the Trinity of the Father, Son and Holy Ghost.

Our settlement, though of the vast majority of Presbyterians in Scotland, is not complete ; we would rejoice to see with us brethren who are still separate. This latest and largest union is not the last, either with others of our own system or with those from whom we must be content at present to be more or less ecclesiastically separate ; they are not far from us, and they show a cordial interest in our Union. Our promise to be ready to explore the situation indicated in the Lambeth proposals stands ; but this is a very different question from what we have now settled. Dean Stanley said : " There is much to be said for Presbyterianism, much for Episcopacy, but much more for the

secondary, temporary, accidental character
of both, when compared with the general
principles to which they each minister."
Meantime let us create an atmosphere that
will prepare for a closer fellowship, by distinguishing between articles necessary for
grace and order, and those necessary for
salvation.

The next section of the address reviewed
the Church's tasks.   Foremost is the moral,
social and religious well-being of the Scottish
people.   The churchless million is the first
challenge.   Great things are required if the
Church is to win them back to the faith of
their fathers.   An encouraging feature is the
conspicuous service of an increased number
of women of the Church, and in the Plan
of Re-Union fuller recognition is accorded
them, while provision is made in guilds and
associations for the various services they can
render.   Something has still to be done for
their aptitude as teachers—a needed ministry
and a development of the order of Deacon-

esses and Church Sisters.   Any change must
be made deliberately and without creating
fresh cleavage in the Church.

Related to the Home Mission Problem is
the Church's responsibility to the changed
social conditions. She cannot stand aloof
from the social and economic life of the
nation. Not called to frame schemes, she
can enforce two principles of human value
and comradeship—the equal and infinite
value of every personality in the sight of God,
and the brotherhood of man.   From this the
Moderator passed to international tasks, the
cause of unity in Christendom and the world-
wide mission to which our Lord calls.   He
discussed the Church's hold on the intellectual life of the country and her duty to
correlate to the modern world-view the
unchanging truths of the faith, as her
University schools of theology should help
her to do through an educated ministry.
The critical hour when the Church can help
is when youth is doing its own thinking and

young men and women are making their adjustments to personal problems, society and God. The older members must retain their touch with the progressive forces of life. We need fellowships of study in all our congregations, to learn to love the Lord with all our *mind*, and rethink the teaching of our Faith. The priesthood of knowledge and the intellect cannot be divorced from that of believers.

His final word was that the Church is more than organisation—a living organism which should be the pulsing Body of Christ under Him alone. Acts of Parliament and Assembly indicate the orderly relations of Church and State, but the strength and safeguard of the Church are from within, relying on the fountain of Apostolic Life, her establishment in the truth of the Fellowship and Love of God, and her endowment by His Spirit for a united testimony to her Lord and Saviour, which we are assured will win the world. In this faith we go forward.

With one heart the Assembly rose to the Moderator's vision and powerful call upon the Church.

The remaining business of this Diet was the selection of a Committee to prepare an answer to the King, and the following appointments : the Reverend Doctors J. T. Cox and James Harvey as Senior Clerks, and J. G. Sutherland as Junior Clerk, of Assembly, and of Dr. William Chree as Procurator, to all of whom the oath *de fideli* was administered ; of J. A. S. Millar, A. H. M'Lean and E. J. M'Candlish as Law Agents of the Church ; of A. H. Spens as Parliamentary Solicitor, and A. B. Noble as Custodier of Titles ; of A. Yellowlees and J. T. S. Watson as the General Treasurers and J. M'Kerrell Brown and D. N. Cotton as Auditors. The Standing Orders of the Assembly were approved, and the House confirmed the continuance of the General Trustees of the United Free Church. A Committee was formed to report on the

L

nomination of a Moderator for the General Assembly of 1930, and we adjourned till the evening.

THE EVENING SESSION

An hour before the time the vast hall, warm and well lit, was filled to its extremities by ministers and members of the Church, men and women, with the guests from other Churches, all as earnest and eager as they had been during the afternoon. The sight of that multitude was again overwhelming.

After the opening exercises, in which Psalm lxix. 30, 32-36 was sung, Dr. Sutherland, the Junior Clerk, read a number of messages. The first was from the Prime Minister : " May I send you this word of greeting on an occasion which, both in its immediate significance and its effects, must be of interest to all who have the welfare of Scotland at heart, and who care for its glorious religious traditions. The day of

Re-union will, I hope, be remembered as one of the most notable landmarks in Scottish history, and all Scotsmen will join with me in the fervent hope that the reunited Church will use its power and influence to make religion a continuing strength in the Scottish character, and Presbyterianism a vital form of national worship.—J. Ramsay MacDonald." This from the Earl of Balfour : " Deeply regret I cannot be with you on an occasion which must ever be memorable. I rejoice to have lived to see accomplished the Union I have so earnestly desired. It will give added strength to the Scottish Church, and not in Scotland only."

Others followed :—from the Ladysmith Presbyterians in far Natal, " Our congratulations and prayers are with you " ; from the Church in still further Formosa, " Rejoice with you, greater works than these shall you do " ; from the General Assembly of the Church in China, " Greetings, may your united Church achieve considerable spiritual conquest in Scotland, Chinese situation demands a forward movement, we pledge loyal co-operation " ; and from the United Committee on Methodist Union and the Methodist Conferences, " Hearty congratulations and earnest prayers for the Divine Blessing on the first Assembly." Many other Churches and Societies sent greetings of goodwill :—the Upper House of the Convocation of York, the Welsh Presbyterian and Methodist Churches, the Scottish Episcopal Church, the Society of Friends, the Wesleyan Methodist Church in Scotland, the Free Church and the Baptist Union of Scotland, the General of the Salvation Army, with messages from New Zealand, Switzerland, Alsace-Lorraine, India, Canada, Africa, Australia, Manchuria, and other parts of the world.

We heard and felt that long list as the devout multitude at Pentecost must have heard and felt the representatives from the races of their far smaller world speak in

" our tongues the wonderful works of God."

The Moderator then received and welcomed the Delegates from other Churches and public bodies ; those from the Cities and the Universities of Scotland ; the two eminent Churchmen from the sister National Church, neither a stranger to the Church of Scotland, and received gladly as they look unto the rock whence they were hewn ; Presbyterian brethren from many lands, England, Wales, Ireland, Canada, Australasia, South Africa and the United States, reminding us that our Presbyterian system is international ; delegates from the Scottish Episcopal Church, with which we share many spiritual experiences ; Methodist, Congregational and Baptist friends, to whom we are indebted for the expression of a unity across the dividing lines of all their Churches ; and the delegates from the Churches of the Continent, to which whatever happened, as they heroically faced the political and ecclesiastical difficulties in the new nations, was of deep concern to us. To one and all a most cordial welcome !

The Lord Provost of Edinburgh and the Principal of the University of Aberdeen then addressed the Assembly on behalf of the municipal and academic life of Scotland, the former on the Church's training for and influence upon public affairs ; the latter— after an assurance that the four Universities were in heart with the Union—appealing to the Christian homes of the country to furnish the Church through the Universities with more of their sons for the ministry.

The " Angels of the Churches " followed, sixteen in all, who not only carried the congratulations of their Churches upon the Union, but wisely reminded us of what was still lacking. They were, as was meet, headed by the Archbishop of Canterbury, who brought " greeting and goodwill from the Chair of Augustine to you who reverence Ninian, Kentigern and Columba," as well as a message from both Houses of the Convocation of Canterbury, a message of "thankfulness to God for this new stage in that Re-Union of Christendom to which the Holy Spirit is moving the Church throughout the world." His Grace continued : "The Church of England shares with you the responsibilities of a National Church, called to express the nation's acknowledgment of the Kingdom of God and to minister to the nation the Gospel of Truth and Grace. We cannot but admire and envy the spiritual freedom which in your case the State has acknowledged more fully than ever as the right of the Church. Knowing the loss we suffer by the separation from us of so many of our fellow-Christians, we thank God we are now united with them as never before in a fellowship of common service to His Kingdom, but we long for a closer communion in Faith and Order. This Union of yours is only a beginning. Among other currents of Scottish Christianity still to be brought into the one stream, small yet carrying its own traditions, is the Scottish Episcopal Church. And there is the larger hope that *all* who confess Christ as Lord may be joined in one visible fellowship. Given such able leadership and such faith as have prevailed over your formidable difficulties, who shall say that the even greater difficulties and differences in the way of that Unity may not be overcome ? But this shall be not by large and dramatic movements but step by step, here a little and there a little, Church by Church, in this island or overseas."

His Grace closed with a more personal word which deeply stirred the Assembly. " Not only because I represent the Church of England or am pledged to the cause of Christian Unity is my heart moved, but because I am a Scotsman and a son of the manse, born and bred in the Church of Scotland. . . . I come back with unalterable veneration for the Church of my fathers. I can remember as a boy seeing with mingled

THE UNION GATHERING

interest and awe the leaders of the last
generation, Phin, Scott, Charteris, Story,
Caird, Macgregor and John Macleod ; and
the names of the great teachers of the other
Presbyterian Churches were as household
words. . . . I seem to see among them my
own dear and honoured father. The emotions which rise as I think of him—as perhaps
he thinks of me—are too deep for tears, too
strong for speech. I can only say that to his
son it is a pleasure that the signal honour of
being the first Moderator of this Assembly
should have been given to his successor in
the Barony. You will forgive these personal
words. How could I forbear from speaking
them ? . . . May the celebration of your
unity quicken our faltering steps in the quest
of the city of our dreams—the One, Holy
Catholic Church."

From the Archbishop of Canterbury to
the Original Secession !—the passage was
one of the most striking moments of the
Assembly. Bearing greetings from all the

other Scottish Presbyterians, the Reverend Professor Morton directly represented the first break from the national Church of Scotland in 1733, when the Seceders' appeal had been (as he said) back to the first free and reforming Assembly of that Church. But this also was a free Assembly which the Secession and Disruption Fathers would have rejoiced to see. The Moderator's ideal of the union of all the Scottish streams still outside was deeply impressive, and he hoped it would be realised. This day meant very much for the religious life of Scotland, and he prayed the Blessing of God on her re-united Church.

The following Moderators of the other Presbyterian Churches in the United Kingdom then spoke. Dr. P. J. Maclagan, of the Presbyterian Church of England, after re-calling that the Scottish *Confession, Catechisms* and metrical Psalms had their origin on English soil, and owning the debt of his Church to the Churches in Scotland for ministers and members, said that her representatives were profoundly moved by the proceedings of these days, and from their own experiences of union could see how this one was bound to become still closer with the years.   As a missionary he knew what it meant throughout the world in setting free resources and re-opening the springs of spiritual life.   From the Presbyterian Church of Wales, " a little country whose greatest achievement was great preaching," Mr. R. R. Roberts appealed for the maintenance of doctrinal training and proclamation of the pure Gospel.   Let the younger ministers be done with the note of uncertainty and dedicate their hereditary theological skill and Celtic passion to making the next step after Union the revival of earnest evangelical preaching.   And Dr. J. L. Morrow of Clontarf, claiming his Church as a daughter of the Church of Scotland, recalled how her first congregation was instituted in Ireland almost 300 years ago by Church of Scotland

Chaplains to the troops in Carrickfergus, and how the present Presbyterian Church of Ireland was formed 89 years back by the Union of the Synods of Ulster and the Secession. " Beside him on the platform was his brother the Bishop of Cashel from the Church of Ireland, and they two might be taken as speaking for the whole Protestant population of that country. They prayed for the Church of Scotland the full realisation of the ideals of those who had promoted her Union. He thought it fitting that Saint Patrick should be there to bless Saint Columba." The Moderator of the Free Church of Scotland, unable to be present, had sent a message.

The next whom the House welcomed, and right heartily, was the Primus of the Scottish Episcopal Church, Bishop W. J. F. Robberds, D.D. To the congratulations of all the Scottish Bishops, who thanked God for this Union and prayed that the re-united Church might be abundantly blessed to His

Glory, he added that for himself, who had first-hand knowledge of the progress towards Union during these twenty years, as to all Scotsmen, the movement had been a matter of the deepest interest, concern and personal sympathy. This solemn moment could not but open up vistas of larger hopes, and in ways as yet unseen Scotland might witness a still wider unity.

Next came the honoured messages from the Free Churches of England and their Irish brethren. Dr. J. H. Ritson, London, said that the Wesleyans, hoping for their own Union with the Primitive and United Methodists by 1932, were watching this Scottish one with peculiar interest. Many dreamt, too, of a Union of Presbyterianism and Methodism, near relations with good gifts for each other. Till that came let us never forget that the Church's strength was not her size but her spiritual life. Principal Garvie, with addresses from the Federated Council of the Free Churches of England,

and the National Free Church Council, venturing also to represent the Irish Congregationalists, assured us of their hearty joy in our Union ; and added that as a Scotsman, like the Archbishop of Canterbury, he rejoiced with all Scotsmen that Scotland was showing such an example to the world with the promise it held of a re-union of all Christendom.   Mr. M. E. Aubrey, London, for the Baptist Union of Great Britain and Ireland, gave thanks for the service of the Scottish Churches by their wide scholarship, faithful preaching and training of a noble ministry which had succeeded in blending the light of new knowledge with evangelical fervour.   The two denominations had much in common.   He and his fellow-Baptists were not fully persuaded of the relations of Church and State involved in the Union, and would carefully watch results.   This shadow of difference threw into relief their goodwill and rejoicing in the mending of a broken fellowship—a gift from God.

Voices from over the seas then spoke to us.
Dr. George C. Pidgeon, Toronto, told of the
delight in our Union felt by the United
Church of Canada, enjoying the Methodist
and Congregational heritages as well as the
Presbyterian. If the Church of Scotland,
after exploring the situation, could find a
safe direction towards a wider Union, this
would bring the fulfilment of their Master's
Prayer nearer by generations than their
fathers had dreamed. Dr. David Perrie,
Moderator of the Presbyterian Church of
Canada, said they realised that only in Scotland could such a Union have been effected.
As Marcus Dods said, Christianity's stiffest
fight against the forces of evil and indiffer-
ence would come in the twentieth century.
For that battle let us stand shoulder to
shoulder ! Dr. Ronald G. M'Intyre bore the
greetings of the Churches of Australia and
New Zealand, outposts of the Presbyterian
faith, with reverent affection for their
Mother-Church, now the freest in the

Empire, to whom her children in the Dominions look to keep her old place in the van of all that makes for the Kingdom of God. Dr. Bulloch Douglas, East London, for the English-speaking Church in South Africa, which drew her whole ministry and membership from her Scottish Mother, and for the native Bantu Church, reminded us that the Dutch Reformed Church, with sixty per cent. of the people, is also Presbyterian. Throughout the land the Scottish Re-Union was hailed with immense sympathy and heartfelt congratulations.

The last three messengers to us were from Churches beyond the British Empire, in Europe and America. Professor Kováts, Budapest, representing the Reformed Churches of Europe, uttered the prayers " of many millions of hearts," that to all who share in our Union it may serve for the growth of their faith and love to God, unto His Glory. This duty had fallen to a Hungarian because of the historical connections between the Christianity of Scotland and that of Hungary—through the saintly Queen Margaret nearly nine centuries ago, through the sacrifices of Scots soldiers in the relief from the Turks of the fortress of Buda, that outpost of Christendom, and through the privilege God had given the Scottish Churches for the last fifty years in the spiritual awakening of the oldest Presbyterian Church on the Continent. He himself learned the real power of Christianity at New College, Edinburgh.

Bishop Johan Lunde, Primate of the Evangelical Lutheran Church of Norway, brought the fraternal greetings of all the Lutherans of Europe, but especially of his own Church, as also of His Majesty King Haakon VII, a very interested friend of all Christian work. The Scottish Isles were once a Norwegian diocese ; the two peoples, brothers in blood as in faith, have in common some features of character. May the Church of Scotland

M

maintain the heroic spirit of her fathers and shine for all the world !

Introducing the Hon. John Finley, an editor of the *New York Times*, the Moderator said it was appropriate that the last speaker should be an elder. Colonel Finley, addressing the Assembly as " the fellow-countrymen of my ancestors," called the Presbyterian Church " Scotland's greatest gift to America." The eighteen thousand Presbyterian congregations in the States, with three and a quarter million members, were divided into *thirteen* different bodies, but this Scottish Union stirred hopes that they also will move towards unity, like the *thirteen* original States of America, who, composing their differences, symbolised their Federation in the motto (of *thirteen* letters) *E Pluribus Unum*. More than half of the framers of that Federation were of Scottish blood or of Scottish training, and of the Presbyterian Faith. To-day Scotland and America are nearer than ever. " I bring you most cordial greetings from the Land of Youth, of which your earliest bards have sung, and which this week will be rediscovered by the Scottish helmsman of your great ship of State." [1]

Thus the memorable Day of Scottish Re-Union was gloriously crowned by an evening of Catholic communion, rejoicing and hopes, unprecedented in our own, or perhaps in any, national history.

The Second Day

The General Assembly opened the next day of their Session, Thursday, 3rd October, with the Sacrament of the Lord's Supper in St. Giles, when, as on the day before, the sacred simplicity of the Presbyterian rite blended with the faith and vision of the whole Catholic Apostolic Church. The Moderator presided, opening the Service with the Forty-third Psalm, " O send Thy

[1] A reference to the Prime Minister's American visit.

Light forth and Thy Truth," to its own
Scottish tune of " Invocation."   Prayer and
readings of the Word followed, the Nicene
Creed was recited, we sang our hymn of
approach to the Table, Paraphrase xxxv.,
the Words of Institution were read, and after
thanksgiving, adoration and prayer for the
Holy Spirit to " bless and consecrate the
Gifts of Bread and Wine, to be unto us the
Communion of the Body and Blood of
Christ, to our spiritual nourishment and
growth in grace," the Sacrament was dis-
pensed by the Minister to the Elders and by
the Elders distributed to the Members, sitting as they partook, according to our
immemorial fashion as (in Knox's words)
" approaching most ney to Christis awin
actioun."   By prayer our hearts were lifted
to the Communion of Saints and, by the
opening verses of Psalm ciii. upon the notes
of " Coleshill," in full thanks to God Himself.   None who partook of this Sacrament
can ever forget its solemn service in the Kirk

of our fathers with the thoughts recalled of God's mercies and the dear memories stirred of those with whom of old we had kept holy day.

Carrying these thoughts and memories we were out again among the crowds, who as yesterday thronged the approaches to the Assembly Hall, and once more proved how closely our countrymen were with us.

The first business of the day was the submission and approval of the Assembly's loyal and grateful reply to the King's Letter, rejoicing in His Majesty's recovery, with the prayer that He may long be spared to His people ; welcoming the renewed appointment of the Duke of York to represent His Majesty ; thankfully acknowledging the assurance of His Majesty's concern for the maintenance of the rights and liberties of the Church of Scotland ; and praying for the Blessing of Almighty God upon the King, the Queen and all the Royal House.

On behalf of the National Bible Society, their President, Lord Maclay, presented the Moderator with a Bible for the use of himself and his successors, the Burning Bush on its cover and the date of the Union on its title-page, " to be a perpetual reminder to future generations of the new era which dawned on Scotland in 1929." The Directors of the Society hoped " that this Bible might be the symbol that our great Scottish Church based its doctrine, creed and worship on ' The Word of God that liveth and abideth for ever.' "

In accepting the Book, the Moderator said it was needed to constitute the Assembly ; their deliberations centred around it, and they hoped it would be more and more reinstated in the homes of the people of Scotland.

The Assembly then addressed themselves to the tasks awaiting the Church, in four resolutions. The first was on the Church's

missionary duty at home.   In moving this,
Dr. Harry Miller said it consisted of two
resolutions and a reminder : first, to prose-
cute with new energy, not only among the
poor but among the rich, home-mission and
evangelistic work, for the two Churches had
joined under the pressure of a deep sense of
their duty in the fight against materialism
and the desire to gauge human life in terms
of material possessions or of the lack of them,
and against the social evils of bad housing,
drunkenness and gambling ; second, to inspire the youth of the land by the ideals in
which the well-springs of our national history
are to be found ; and following this, to
remind our members of their duty and
privilege to be the messengers of God to
their families and their neighbours.   For the
many who had been brought in not only by
ministers of the Church but by the more
powerful influences of their homes, this reminder was the leading thing in the resolution.   In seconding, Lord Polwarth, after a

tribute to his father and Dr. Charteris, said
that in every parish are found the indifferent,
respectable citizens, to whom it made no
difference that Christ lived and died for
them, and who seldom or never went to
church. Each Kirk Session or Presbytery
must survey its own area, find means through
ministers, but the laity as well, to take the
Church's message to every one within its
bounds. Special missions by those of special
gifts would be required. The Church must
never deem any one too bad or sunken for
it to stretch out a hand in the Master's
Name.

The second resolution enforced the duty
of the Church to the non-Christian peoples,
with messages of affection and assurance to
the missionaries labouring among them.

Speaking to this, Dr. Donald Fraser said
their fathers saw the crown rights of Jesus in
the light of ecclesiastical loyalties, but we
in that of personal, social and international
loyalties—that Christ should be King to

every man and woman and in all human
relations. True nationalism expressed itself in internationalism. They charged
their sons and daughters abroad to maintain by purity of life the standards which
made their nation great, and to be witnesses
of Christ's Gospel to their fellow-countrymen and other races. The first necessity
of a Catholic Church was union, not only
with past ages but with the races and
nations of to-day. In place of one missionary 100 years ago, Dr. Duff, we have now
788, with more than 7000 native pastors,
teachers and evangelists, and a Christian community of over 338,000 ; besides
48 missionaries to the Jews, with, in the past
twelve years, 40,000 Jews joining the Christian Church. And all these had their gifts
for our Church in return, showing her in
India, Manchuria and Africa the way to
union. If disunion at home was weakness,
in face of heathendom it was a crime. He
eloquently reviewed the moral and social

influences of the Cross in heathen lands. Mr. C. W. G. Taylor, Edinburgh, in seconding, asked, as they thanked God for the triumph of His Spirit over the forces of evil among non-Christian peoples, had not their faith been strengthened that by the same Spirit their difficulties at home might all be solved ?   This would be a new day for Scotland only as they made it the beginning of a new day for the world. Recalling the decay of the once living Church of North Africa, he said the Church which ceased to be evangelistic would ultimately cease to be evangelical.

The third resolution recorded the Assembly's gratitude to God for the consecrated women who have devoted their lives to the service of their Lord at home and abroad, and for the continued development of women's work in the Church, and enjoined ministers and kirk sessions to foster the organised work of women in the Church.

The mover, Dr. Norman Maclean, moved also our hearts by recalling the spirit of Scotswomen, who deemed no sacrifice too great for Christ's Crown and Covenant, and the saintliness and devotion which the Women's Guild and Order of Deaconesses had evolved, in such women as Lady Grizell Baillie, the first Deaconess, and her grand-niece, the Hon. Katherine Scott, of whose service as Police Sister he told an inspiring tale ; also the work of Miss Beck at Blantyre in training girls, and the help given by her sisters, a dressmaker and a teacher at home. " The washtub was a sacramental vessel for Miss Beck, and, her day's work done, he could see her preparing an aged leper for baptism." The soul of Scotland was safe in the hands of Scotland's womanhood. In seconding the resolution, Dr. P. D. Thomson said that in keeping with it was the presence on the platform of a lady over ninety years, Mrs. Bannerman of Perth, who was present at the Disruption, and whom he hailed as an example of noble womanhood and womanly service in the Church. From the women of the Gospels to those of the Church to-day service has been inspired by loyalty to Him whose love for us is wonderful, passing the love of women. It includes the service of women missionaries at home and abroad, doctors, Church sisters, heads of Women's and Girls' Associations and Guilds, women deacons and managers in our congregations, women collectors, and, last but not least, the women of the manse, wives, daughters, mothers and sisters of the regular ministry. Their service is beyond all reckoning and praise. It will be for the Church to watch carefully how that service may be further widened and those gifts utilised which are women's peculiar glory.

Miss Lamond, of Edinburgh, then spoke for the 60,000 members of the Women's Guild over whom she presides, and for other women workers. They are worthy of a greater share in the Church's counsels than has been given them.   She was thankful we had a John White and not a John Knox in the Chair, else would there be not a few Marys and certainly many Marthas in tears. An organisation was wanted to bind all the others, keeping the balance between their various interests and eliminating rivalry. They knew the woman in their congregations who did not wish to see her money go out of the country (meaning her own parish), and on the other hand they had Mrs. Jellyby—it might be in an attenuated form —at every missionary meeting.   They had to rouse the imagination and sympathy of the one and restrain the zeal of the other. That was part of the work of the Women's Guild, in which from the parish branch through the Presbyterial Council to the Central Committee of Management, reporting to the General Assembly, every member of the Guild was linked to the Moderator— though she had not heard of any brought before him for reprimand !   The Guild was also a force uniting the women of Wick with the women of Wigtown, the women of Glasgow with the women of Edinburgh—a more difficult business !—the women of the Western Isles with those of the Eastern sea-board, and the women of Orkney and Shetland with the women of the industrial towns and the pastoral districts of the borders.   And lastly, the Guild was a practical organisation on a deeply religious foundation with a spiritual outlook and atmosphere—not believing in faith without works, and still less in works that were not the outcome of faith.

The last resolution, acknowledging with devout thankfulness the goodness and the guidance of God in the Union which has now been accomplished, and mindful of the longings of the Churches in all lands for unity and concord, exhorted ministers and office-bearers and members to co-operate with their brethren of other Churches in all good works ; to seek the things which make for love and peace ; and to abound in prayer for the unity of the Church of Christ.

This, said Professor Paterson, pledged the Assembly to advance to a wider unity. We shall first try to do our duty by those Churches which are our near relations or neighbours. Of the former are the Reformed : no ignoble family, for it made history in Switzerland and Holland, and includes the heroic Huguenots and Waldenses ; and no small family, for it includes the Presbyterian Churches overseas in our Empire and America. Nor may we forget our kinship with the Church of Martin Luther, which in the sixteenth century sent us the gospel and in the nineteenth enriched our thought. We have special obligations to some who are bone of our bone and flesh of our flesh. One is the Original Secession Church, with whom after Dr. Morton's speech we may expect a speedy reconciliation. Near also are the Free Presbyterians, and the Free Church ; who does not pray for the day when the Church of Scotland shall be enriched by the full volume of Highland piety? We also hope that the separation of those who from conscientious scruples have remained outside us will be only temporary. In the meantime let us cultivate spiritual communion with all such—say, first by a yearly devotional conference and sitting down together at the Table of the Lord. Reviewing past relations with the Episcopal Churches, he said it was possible with our special ecclesiastical experience to suggest a concordat between Episcopacy and Presbytery. But, as the Archbishop had said, the advance must be step by step, the ecumenical councils having chiefly served to bring out the magnitude of the obstacles to be overcome. But we must ever cherish the vision of a unified Christendom. Colonel Roxburgh, LL.D., the Glasgow elder, in seconding, said that it was on the laymen and especially on the office-bearers of the Church that the burden of the action called

for would chiefly lie in cultivating the spirit
of love and charity among all sections.   The
Re-United Church claimed no monopoly
privileges, but to dwell in friendship with all
other Churches.   This is a free Church and
holds itself free to co-operate or unite with
any other.   The difficulties at the beginning
of our own negotiations seemed insurmount-
able, but one by one they had been cleared
out of the way and we now stood united,
anxious only for the Christian good of Scotland ; yet, as the resolution reminded them,
not resting upon what had been accomplished, but keeping before them the wider
outlook.   He was glad to tell the House that
of the £25,000 to be handed over to the Continuing Church something in the neighbourhood of £10,000 had already been raised.

The four resolutions, having been put
successively to the Assembly, were unanimously and cordially passed.

The Assembly then passed Acts on the
Licensing of Probationers, Union of Con-

gregations, Meetings of Presbyteries and Synods and Naming of Congregations ; and made and approved of other arrangements necessary upon the Union ; the Joint Report of the General Committee of the Church of Scotland and Finance Committee of the United Church was submitted and approved, with draft Acts anent Collections and the Budget Committee, which was then appointed ; and *inter alia* Model Deeds of Constitution for existing and new parishes *quoad sacra* were agreed to ; and the House adjourned till the evening.

THREE GREAT ADDRESSES

When the Assembly resumed in the evening under the Moderator and in presence of the Lord High Commissioner, along with the Duchess of York, the vast Hall was again filled, and twelve thousand awaited the addresses promised by eminent leaders of Christian thought and action. They were not disappointed. Three more noble addresses—noble by the courage alike of the truth in which they faced our present world and of their faith and hope in the Church's duties to it—have never been delivered together.

The first was by Dr. Henry Sloan Coffin, President of New York Union Theological Seminary, a native American and an alumnus of New College, Edinburgh. He showed us vividly the civilisation which is fast replacing Christendom, a secular and commercialised civilisation, so dazzled by the achievements of Science as to obscure the presence of God, whose Psychology puts its observations of human behaviour as the basis of conduct in place of religious principles, and whose popular writers offer Humanism to fill the void once filled by God's Revelation of Himself in the Bible and in Christ. East and West alike, no longer possessed by the claims of alternative religions, regard faith in God as a mere sedative for troubled minds or a subject for investigation, but not as needful for vigorous living or a rational interpretation of existence. This he reckoned as not all loss, for Christendom has not applied the Spirit of Jesus to industry, commerce and international relations. There is some despair, but the ineradicable hopefulness of the mass of mankind, and the wistfulness it breeds, are openings for the Church's appeal. What appeal can she make? First, as a worshipping Church. Only the Church to whom God means everything can make Him mean anything to mankind. Second, as a teaching Church, instructing, as the Early Church had to do, a world ignorant of life with Christ in God, witnessing Who He is and how He has revealed Himself, taking the new knowledge which Science has opened up, to inform people how to think of His relation to the Universe ; while not drawing her ethics from Psychology, employing its insight into human behaviour ; training the consciences of her members to bring every aspect of their lives under the Spirit of Christ ; and sending out evangelists who shall also be teachers, persuasively setting forth the Christian message. Third, a Church exemplifying what the Christian life really is by manifesting the Life of her Lord in the morally adventurous lives of her members. And finally, a Church whose fellowship within herself also binds humanity in one. Supranational the true Church of Christ inherently is.

The second address was delivered by Mr. Oldham, honoured for his service to foreign missions and as an expert in the relation of Christianity to race problems and the economic and political conditions of primitive tribes. The world is rapidly becoming a single neighbourhood, by the increasing speed of its means of communication. Its different parts grow more and more interdependent economically, but there is no equivalent growth in human fellowship. The moral task of civilisation is to humanise

the relations of men and increase trust, goodwill and understanding. To conceive the
Church's task in a lesser setting is to lose
touch with reality. Like Dr. Coffin, he
emphasised the transcendent difficulties of
a civilisation based on applied science, the
shocks from which not only the West but the
ancient religions of the East are unable to
stand.   For all men the religious issues grow
more definite. Is there at the heart of the
Universe One Who loves and cares, to
Whom we may pray, a Divine Purpose and
Providential ordering of our lives, as having
a cosmic significance, or is ethic and social
behaviour to be learned only through experi-
ment ? " Make no mistake. Our faith must
re-vindicate its claim to be a faith for the
world, or cease to be a faith for our own
lives." He then surveyed the rapid spread of
industrialism and active education, national
systems of which were springing up in Asia
and Africa. What is the relation of the
Church to these ? " We must think of her

work overseas in a new setting. In this
creative hour let us cast off outworn habits
of thought and accustom our minds to the
truth of the conditions to-day. We cannot
do so without a large, a startling increase of
men, women and money. If the call is to
be met, some of you younger ministers will
have to go." The call is manifold—for a
sustained intellectual effort to think out the
Christian world-view in relation to the whole
range of modern knowledge ; a call to new
adventures in the life of the Spirit, the con-
vincing evidence of the Christian faith being
the power and winsomeness of Christian
lives ; and a call to extend the utmost assist-
ance in our power to the younger weaker
Churches overseas. To meet these calls
Scotland must pour forth of her best. Our
generation at least reverences Christ as real,
as One who faced life unshrinking. Only a
Church that loses herself in the service of the
world, filled with a divine discontent in what
she already is and is doing compared with

the immeasurable tasks ahead, can enter into
life that is life indeed.

To Lord Davidson of Lambeth, for twenty-
five years Primate of England, we rose like
one man.   He said : " I stand here to make
the final speech of two memorable days.
The man must be dull of spirit and feeble of
fibre whose pulse has not been quickened
as he has looked round this hall.   You have
been by God's help healing for good a great
cleavage.   The act is significant, not for
Scotland only but far beyond.   Yes, the act
is significant, and the place and the time are
significant.   Those who have acted are the
citizens of a country wherein Christian
thought, deliberate and keen, is the common
heritage in the homes of the people.   I
know of no land of which that can be so true
as it is here.   Whether we agree or not with
what our people have at different times said
and thought about Church truth and Church
order, we cannot but regard the nature of
these discussions as more or less peculiar to

us Scotsmen—peculiar, because everybody great and small claims to apply individual thought to it. It is quite different from a country's loyal and patient obedience to a Church's rule, right or wrong. See how the usage lives and glows in the Scottish litera-ture of several centuries ! Our act of healing and repair has far greater meaning and significance than it might have in other lands. Every Scotsman has for generations more or less understood for himself questions which would be quite unmeaning to ordinary folk elsewhere. If you will pardon a per-sonal note, I was myself, in years not long after the Disruption, brought up in Scotland, and though I flitted early across the Tweed for training and education and work of quite another kind and allegiance, I have vivid memories of the talk of my elders in those days, and had heard of Auchterarder and Strathbogie long before I can have had a glimmer of what they stood for ; and I re-garded it as a kind of adventure when I was taken once in a way to listen to such men as Candlish and Guthrie at their best. Such memories come flooding in upon me now."

Lord Davidson proceeded to the wider field. For twenty-five years he has held a position nearly unique. The Archbishop of Canterbury is in ceaseless contact with the leaders of Christians across the world, on the St. Lawrence as on the Bosphorus and the Danube, on the Elbe as on the Nile, the Euphrates and the Ganges. Who more fit than he to speak on Christian Unity?

" In the light of our Lord's Prayer," he said, " that Unity cannot be impossible, and if possible surely obligatory. What is the worth of our effort towards it? Neither the thought nor the effort is new, but we have to face new conditions resolutely and squarely, and so we will. Our world grows unified by leaps and strides. Distance is annihilated. Partition walls crumble. There is unity perforce, we are crushed by it. Does Christian Unity come in? Again, what does the League of Nations stand for? People eagerly want peace. Without marring national patriotism we are trying to create one Christian body-politic, so healthy that the war-bacillus, even if it find its way in, shall be harmless. Eight years ago I came to address the Assemblies, straight from the Lambeth Conference, whose published *Appeal to All Christian Peoples* was to reach out towards a Re-United Catholic Church. With one great exception the response has been cordial, hopeful, stimulating, all the world over, incredible as this would have been deemed fifty years ago. We have been stirred by the amazing change in our relation to the Great Churches of the East, which have started sympathies and efforts foreign to them for centuries, and no gathering of European Churches for conference but has been attended by splendid men of learning, devotion and experience, whose fields of work lie in the historic Eastern Patriarchates. There is, of course, one great exception. No helpful word or act comes from the City of the Seven Hills. Members of that Church will not even join us in prayers. Of course they will tell us that the footpath is easy if we will do their bidding. But may I quote words which I ventured to use in speaking to the Assemblies nine years ago ? Moderator, in view of what we see and know of the whole-hearted, faithful, untiring zeal and the quiet devotion of innumerable members of that great society, I wish to God I could modify my words now, but when we are talking of unity I dare not. My words were these : ' We have never ceased to make it clear that we can enter no portal of fellowship which has submission graven on its lintel—submission to what would be unendurable because it is untrue. About that we have no vestige of hesitation. And no path which we could possibly tread upon a reconciliation-road is at present even dimly in sight. Yet as we bow reverently before the Lord, " Who

maketh men to be of one mind in an house,"
and look onward into the unrolling of His
purpose, I dare not myself quite say *Lasciate
ogni speranza*, or hold it inconceivable that,
in the providence of God, a truer light may
some day dawn.' "

Leaving that, Lord Davidson reviewed
the nine years of gatherings at Lambeth of
committees from Non-Episcopal Churches in
England to discuss possibilities and draw-
backs, never without hope of their solution;
conferences in European countries, of which
the Lake of Geneva is the centre for promot-
ing unity, with the League permanently at
Geneva, and at Lausanne two years ago the
Conference on Faith and Order under
Bishop Brent, which sprang as a seedling
from Edinburgh in the final session of the
Missionary Conference of 1910 ; and the
commissions and deputations between England and America, with their reports and
appeals. " You and I," he said, " have
lived through years wherein for the first time

the sundered forces in Christendom, with the exception I have named, have been praying and taking counsel to further His Will. . . . . What you have been doing this week is part, and an important part, of the whole plan at which we are enthusiastically working with one heart and soul. . . . What does it all come to ? What is it all for ? Not merely that it is more brotherly and pleasant to work together, but because of the work before us and the need of tackling it in force. It is so fatally easy to rub along ' forgetting there is a war on ' to the death against the impurities, laziness and greed which corrupt the common life, wherein we as the Church of the Living God are enlisted and united not for rest but for advance. Forward, then, together ! I have said my say. In my eighty-second year I leave with you, my younger brothers, the lesson of hope which these long and busy years have brought to me. I like to think of the ennobling possibilities which await you. It is not we, whose course is well-nigh run, who can bring to accomplishment the vision of Unity which is ours. You can discharge it, and I think you will. Enlist, I pray you, in the great emprise, the vigour of manhood and the buoyancy of youth. May the Lord, Who prayed that all may be one, Himself bless you and keep you this night and all the days that are to come."

CLOSE OF THE ASSEMBLY

The usual Act appointing and empowering a Commission of Assembly was passed. The next General Assembly was ordained to meet on Tuesday, 20th May 1930, and the Reverend Andrew N. Bogle, Doctor of Divinity, was nominated with acclamation as its Moderator ; the House agreeing with his proposers, Professor Paterson and Dr. Drummond, that he needed no argument to commend him, having served his Church and the Union with extraordinary business

capacity and as certain to discharge the high
office with intellectual distinction and spiritual power.

The Moderator then delivered his closing
address. He thanked our Edinburgh hosts,
the Lord Provost and Council, and their
efficient constabulary ; all who had transformed this building, as by Aladdin's Lamp,
into a Hall of Assembly, and the young men
who had acted assiduously as stewards.   He
hailed anew the delegates to the Assembly,
the messengers of the Churches and religious
societies, the civic representatives and other
eminent visitors, whose presence and speeches
had made the occasion still more memorable,
with full promise of a wider Union, and of
the World for Christ.   It remains for us to
see that the Blessings so abundantly poured,
and received with thankfulness to God, are
used with new fidelity, every mercy a call to
duty.   As we bid each other farewell, let our
last thought be of the one real centre of Unity,
Jesus Christ and His indwelling Spirit.

Turning to the Lord High Commissioner, he trusted that His Grace could report favourably to the King upon the proceedings of the court, which dealt with so many issues affecting the Church's efficiency and the religious well-being of the people. This is but the beginning of the work before the United Church, abler than ever, we hope, to contribute its factor to the reconstructive processes of to-day, and by its Gospel to discover the source of peace between man and God, of justice between class and class, and of brotherhood between nation and nation. Our allegiance to the King of Kings makes loyalty to our Sovereign a religious as well as a civil duty. That loyalty has ever been constant ; to-day it is an affectionate loyalty. . . . We thank God for preserving to us on the Christian Throne of this kingdom a Ruler whose kingly character, loving concern for his people and deep interest in the Scottish Church make our allegiance a privilege and joy. The Throne

o

has our confidence ; but the central home of the Empire holds our hearts.   We pray for a rich blessing upon His Majesty, our gracious Queen, and the Royal Family.   And so, in the name of the Assembly, the Moderator bade his Royal Highness farewell.

Replying, the Lord High Commissioner expressed his sense of high privilege in witnessing and sharing the ceremonies which completed the historic Re-Union.   Its significance was enhanced by the presence of delegates from all quarters of Christendom ; what Scotland has achieved will be of influence for Christian Unity throughout the world.   The Moderator and others had referred to the tasks before the Church.   His Grace ventured to think that to all these the Church will go forward from strength to strength.   Its appeal comes with special force to the youth of Scotland ; the Church will make larger demands on their adventurous spirit.   His Grace added that he would convey a favourable report of the Assembly to the King and inform His Majesty that the next General Assembly had been appointed to meet on the twentieth of May 1930. In the King's name he bade us farewell.

The Moderator and members having bowed to His **Grace**, the Moderator, turning to the Assembly, said : " In the Name of the Lord Jesus Christ, sole King and Head of the Church, I now dissolve this General Assembly and appoint the next General Assembly of this Church to be held at Edinburgh on Tuesday the twentieth day of May 1930."

We sang our Psalm of Dismission : " Pray that Jerusalem may have Peace and Felicity," and the Moderator pronounced the Benediction. As we separated we sang the National Anthem.

Amid all the sacred joys of these great days —their precious memories and richer hopes

and visions, our gratitude to our leaders, and
the uplifting of our fellowship in faith and
prayer—the strongest impression upon us as
we left was that of the deeply searching
power of the addresses we had heard.
We came back to the world with a new
conscience of our shortcomings in the past,
and of the tasks awaiting our faith in the
days to come.

THE FUTURE

CHAPTER III

THE FUTURE [1]

I

THE HOPES AND DANGERS OF UNION

" WHOSOEVER in writing a moderne His-torie," Sir Walter Raleigh wrote, " shall follow truth too neare the heeles, it may happily strike out his teeth." It is not easy to judge of the ultimate value of a recent event, since it is not permitted to pry into the future. Both union and disruption have been common in our history, but romance and popular interest have attached them-selves rather to the second than to the first.

[1] In this chapter I have used some sentences from an address given in Edinburgh during the General Assembly of 1929.

It is the memory of our old defiances spoken against England, the first and second Reformations, the drama of 1843, that we have been accustomed to cherish, as if our philosophy were that of Milton's famous words : " By His divorcing command the world first rose out of chaos ; nor can be renewed again out of confusion but by the separating of unmeet consorts."

Yet no consort is so unmeet for the Church as antagonisms which have exhausted their justice. It is better in the long run to build up than to break down, to unite than to sever ; or, rather, destruction and severance are futile except with a view to an ultimate construction and unity. The fault of sectarianism is that it mistakes the means for the end. No doubt dissent needs courage and is often noble and justifiable, but there may be a rarer courage in an insistence upon matters of agreement rather than upon those of difference, and a stronger justification at the bar of history.

What are the dangers of union, for dangers there are ? It may involve, in Stevenson's mocking words, the

lack of a' sectarian füsh'n,
An' cauld religious destitution.

Human affection clings more closely to the smaller unit, as a soldier's love is for his regiment rather than for his brigade, for his division than for his corps. Particularism is apt to evoke the more strenuous loyalties. A man's interest is keenest in what distinguishes him from the mass of his fellows, and his attachment is warmer toward those who are segregated along with himself and to the creed which segregates them. There may be a unison which is attained through a general lack of interest, a weary peace which is based not on a common faith but on a common apathy. No union is of any lasting value in which the whole does not absorb the honest loyalties formerly given to the parts. The only justification for the

breaking down of particularism is a stronger
faith in the fundamentals. Unless the union
of the Churches is attended not merely with
a freedom from contention but with a positive increase of vigour and purpose, far
better was the old sectarianism. The liberty
we need is Burke's liberty, " manly, moral
and regulated," not a bare absence of
bonds but a thing rich in content, a spirit
able and eager to use its new freedom in
new duties.

The circumstances in which union has
been attained entitle us to hope for such a
spirit. For the chief incentive to it has been
a realisation of the new magnitude of the
Church's problem, and the imperative demand in the face of it for the Church to free
itself of encumbrances. Religious energy
must be released from the obsession of lesser
matters—disputes about the niceties of orthodoxy and Church government. The need
to-day is for a race of prophets to arise.
Scotland in the past has produced too many

priests and ritualists, for there may be a
deadly ritualism in a Church which abhors
ritual, since the word means no more than
the setting of the letter above the spirit.
She has produced too many ecclesiastics
who were engrossed in their own sphere, like
devotees of some abstruse science, and had
little regard for the uncovenanted world
around them. The need to-day is for
prophets who will enlarge the sphere of
Christian duty and sharpen its purpose—
men to whom there is nothing secular which
is not also sacred, whose antagonists are not
those of their own household, who in a
slightly different form profess the same faith,
but the eternal enemy, sin and sorrow and
pain—in the words of the Book of Revelation,
" that great city which spiritually is called
Sodom and Egypt, where also our Lord was
crucified."

II

THE PROBLEMS OF THE CHRISTIAN CHURCH

What main problems confront a united Church—confront indeed the whole Church of Christ ?

There is in the first place the question of creed. Religion is not a static thing, the forms of which have been established once for all by a divine decree which admits of no fresh interpretation. It is the spiritual conception of life, and therefore of the universe in which life is lived. But it is independent of any particular cosmogony, and the old divines unfortunately were driven to make a precise cosmogony an essential article of faith. To them, if I may quote what I have written elsewhere, " the earth and all therein were made purposely by God for man, and man's journey heaven-ward or hell-ward was the sole object of creation." They held that " a few thousand years earlier the universe had been fabricated out of chaos in six calendar days, that all history antecedent to our era had been a preparation for the coming of Christ, and that, the supreme sacrifice having been accomplished, at any moment the skies might open, and the trumpets sound, and the short story of earth be closed." This cosmic assurance has crumbled before the advance of science, and to-day our view of the universe has passed far beyond such anthropocentric fancies. We see our earth, which once seemed half the cosmos, an inconsiderable planet revolving with an infinity of others in the immensity of space. We have learned that human life has relations through countless aeons with lower existences, and is kin alike to the brutes and to the stars. The universe has become stranger than any poet's dream, in the deserts of hyper-space the human mind is still blindly groping, and physical science, which a few generations ago was confident about all things in heaven and earth, now uncovers its head humbly in the presence of mysteries which it cannot fathom and can scarcely define.

In the face of this new modesty of science theology dare not be too dogmatic. We realise that it, too, is not a static thing, and that antiquarian accretions are no part of its essence. Theology is an attempt to systematise the divine revelation and to bring it into accord with every aspect of life. But life varies and enlarges its content, and the divine effluence which illuminates it must pass through new lenses. The essentials of our religion can never change. There is still for every man the choice of two paths ; conversion in its plain evangelical sense is still the greatest fact in any life ; Bunyan's mountain gate has still to be passed, which " has room for body and soul, but not for body and soul and sin." Man must still be brought into direct communion with his Maker, and the only comfort in sorrow and pain is that he should know that his Re-

deemer liveth. The prime task of religion
is to spiritualise life, and in this task its foe
is not science and the questioning powers
of the mind, for science itself is a spiritual
activity. The danger comes from the appli-
cation of science, which has so marvellously
elaborated the mechanical apparatus of life,
and may lead to an undue exaltation of
mechanism. To counteract this peril there
is need of a simpler and intenser evangel,
freed from the lumber of a theology which
itself may be a mechanical thing.

But the insistence upon the eternal sim-
plicities of the faith will not lead us to any
shallow contempt for the work of our predecessors. The doctrine of relativity holds
good in this as in other spheres. A formula,
which was once a potent revelation, may
seem to us an empty echo, but in its own day
it may have been a just and fruitful interpretation. The duty of restatement is always
with us, and our own interpretation will be
revised by our children. There is no dis-

charge in the eternal struggle to adjust the
spirit of man to the world by bringing his
material environment within the spiritual
orbit.   If we seek a definition of this creed
we shall find it in one who was contemporary
with our own Covenanters, the Puritan
Isaac Penington.   "All truth," he wrote,
" is shadow except the last truth.   But all
truth is substance in its own place, though it
be but a shadow in another place.   And the
shadow is a true shadow, as the substance
is a true substance."

Secondly, there is the problem of conduct.
It is idle to deny that to-day there is a
general loosening of moral sanctions, as our
fathers understood them.   Certain props to
conventional ethics have gradually fallen
away—the old tradition of church attend-
ance, of Sabbath observance, of Bible reading.   There is a good deal of moral anarch-
ism abroad, due partly to the importance
acquired by the mere mechanism of life, and
partly to the popularising of half-understood

philosophic doctrines about the right of each
man to self-realisation and the development
of the personality. The social discipline,
which insisted upon a general norm of
conduct, has been gravely weakened. The
disintegration apparent in so much modern
art and thought is not less prominent in
morals.

Much of this is to the good. Pharisaism,
the fidelity to conventions which have lost
any binding spiritual force, is no basis for
virtue. Moral sanctions need revision and
adjustment as much as intellectual beliefs.
Men alter their moral codes as they alter
the fashion of their clothes ; witch-hunting
and intolerance were once outward proofs
of godliness, and slave-owning was not held
to be inconsistent with humanity. The
Church has the duty in such questions of
facing frankly changed conditions, and
bringing the light of its revelation to bear
on new perplexities.

But, along with this obligation to examine

P

problems honestly and to reject embargoes
which have become meaningless, goes an
obligation to insist upon the need of moral
discipline—that broad, rational and humane
morality which is the teaching of Christ.
The revolt of young anarchy is less against
Christ's mandates than against what it regards as the perversion of them by official
interpreters.　Disintegration is not a mood
in which the world can long abide, and it is
the Church's task to build up a new and
wiser discipline, to " guard the fire within "
though the " carved gods " have to be left
behind.

It is a task which to some extent must
bring it into contact with the State, for
in the present organisation of society the
State must provide a legal and social back-
ground to private ethics.　If on the part of
the civil government there is the duty to
recognise religion, there is a not less binding
duty upon a national Church to advise and
support the government in providing the

civic sanctions for Christian morality. " I am more and more of a mind," Robert Baillie wrote, " that churchmen, be they never so abill, are unhappie statesmen " ; but there is one province of statesmanship where the Church has both the right and the duty to intervene.

In the third place, missionary enterprise has acquired in the post-war world a new meaning. It is a happy omen that the year of Union was also the centenary of the recognition by the Scottish Church of its missionary duty by the sending out of Alexander Duff to India. The development of transport and communications has brought the world closer. The War taught us that every part subtly reacts upon the rest, that all peoples are members one of another, and that the peace and prosperity of a nation may be linked organically with the peace and prosperity of remote lands. The loose, embryonic society of an older world has gone for ever, and to-day myriads

of human souls depend for their very existence upon the mechanism of civilisation
working in all parts of the globe with
smoothness and security.

Under such conditions missionary work
takes on a new meaning. It can no longer
be treated as a *parergon* of the Christian
Church ; it is one of its most urgent practical duties. One gain from the tragedy of
war has been a recognition of the vital
interest of each country in the well-being of
others, however far distant in space ; and
another is the slow dawning of a true internationalism, which seeks to add to the
patriotisms of races and nations a patriotism
of humanity. Now, world peace depends
in the long run upon a universal will to
peace rather than upon sanctions and
treaties, upon a change of heart and a new
code of values, upon the general acceptance
and practice of the rules of Christian ethics.
The missionary has always been the advance
guard of civilisation, but to-day he is some-

thing more. He is not a lonely figure, representative of a special communion, doing his work sometimes in opposition to, generally in isolation from, the secular activities of his countrymen. He is a vital part of the new civil service of peace, and the tasks at which he labours are the same as those which from another angle are undertaken by chanceries and diplomatists. The missionary side of the Church is " established," in fact if not in law, because it works in the same province and to the same end as the civil power.

Lastly, there is the eternal problem of the society in which we live, a society which through the growth of population and the interweaving of economic interests has developed problems of infinite complexity and desperate urgency, and which reveals, along with many potentialities of hope, many dark certainties of evil. Our view of the State has moved far to-day from the old Victorian detachment. We realise that the central

unity, which is the nation in its corporate
character, must do more than keep the lists
clear for individual effort : that it has in
certain matters a direct duty, which it alone
can fulfil, to supplement, and in some cases
override, the private activities of its citizens.
This richer conception of the State is accompanied by a quicker conscience in the
individual. We no longer believe that
human misery is the result of some mysteri-
ous decree of Omnipotence ; we realise that
it is mainly the consequence of human
bungling. Nor do we consider that we can
shoulder the whole burden of its relief upon
any government ; we recognise a personal
obligation. This seems to me, among so
many losses, one solid and indubitable gain.
Of this duty the Church must be the inspirer
and the interpreter. Its business is not only
with eternity but with time, to enable men
to live worthily and not merely to die in
hope, and to build upon earth the Kingdom
of God.

In such a task it has one prophet to show the way. Just as in the case of our greater statesmen party labels are soon forgotten, so Thomas Chalmers stands to us to-day less as the leader of the Disruption and the founder of a new Church, than as the supreme religious genius of modern Scotland. His masculine intellect made him a scholar in many spheres ; he was a famous orator and a sagacious ecclesiastic ; his character was wholly pure and benevolent, and he was as simple and modest as Sir Walter Scott. But, above all, he was that rare thing, a true national leader, who lifted his countrymen to a higher spiritual level and opened vistas that but for him had been sealed. He insisted on applying the spirit of the Evangel to the whole economy of the land. Had he been born in the days of the first Reformers he would have been as careless of his life as any, for courage was the breath of his being, but he had to deal with things more unnerving than " dag or dagger." To me he seems the greatest constructive mind that the Scottish Church has produced, and one of the noblest figures in any Church—as far above Knox in vision and wisdom as he surpassed him in charity.

III

THE PROBLEMS OF SCOTLAND

The tasks which I have enumerated are common to all branches of the Church of Christ. But there are certain others which specially confront the Church of Scotland.

That Church, as we have seen, has always been most intimately and organically linked to Scottish life. For at least three centuries it was the most living thing in the land. It was the pioneer in popular education. It provided for long the only means by which the ordinary man could make his voice heard on public questions. It led the way in social service, and it played an honourable part during the difficult time when the Highlands, with their traditional social structure in ruins, were faced with the grievous problem of accommodating themselves to an alien world. It did much to show the road to industrial and rural development ; from many country manses came a stimulus to scientific agriculture, the wife of the minister of Kilmaurs founded the Paisley thread manufacture, and the minister of Galashiels was one of the pioneers of the Border tweed trade. Its influence upon the people was incalculable, for its teaching coloured their whole outlook on life. Take the Church and the Bible away from Scottish literature since the Reformation, and how much of that literature is left ? Scottish thought, even when it was vehemently anti-theological, owed most of its forms and categories to the generations behind it of acute theological interest.

It is a platitude that Scotland is changing fast—has changed, indeed, within living memory into a land where the ghosts of other days would recognise little that was familiar.   Novelties have arisen which bring with them new problems, and many former things have passed, or are passing, away.

Chief of these new things was the Industrial Revolution, which came to Scotland in as violent a form as the Reformation. The balance of town and country was wholly upset, and one half of the population was crowded into the valley of a single river. The midlands became a hive of industry, villages grew into towns, towns into cities, and cities into sprawling wens.   There was no foresight, no conscience ; and men, who on the Sabbath were props of their kirks, were blindly busy all the week in activities which took hope and sunlight out of human life.   The housing conditions thus created were among the most hideous in the world, and the problem, before the country was awake to it, had become almost insoluble. Men and women were herded into insanitary

new barracks, or into the old, overcrowded
tenements of Glasgow and Edinburgh.
Those tall stone dwellings do not tumble
down, they have an awful continuing power,
and to-day make a Scottish slum one of the
grimmest sights in Europe.   The result was
sickly children and stunted men and women.
Moreover, the haste to get rich had led
masters to import and exploit cheap alien
labour, Irish and Continental, and to-day
one-eighth of the people of Scotland are
Irish in race and Roman Catholic in creed
—a proportion yearly increasing.

From such a fermenting vat strange
vapours might be looked for.   The brutality
and insecurity of industrial conditions made
Scotland a laboratory for the generation of
social policies.   Like the Covenanters, men,
finding their world insufferable, dreamed of
a new world where the mighty would be
humbled and the lowly exalted, and the
creed thus brought to birth was held with
the fervour of a religion.   Scotland has

become a home of the extreme doctrines of social revolution. It matters little that these doctrines may be impracticable and unsound ; the fact to be faced is that they have only too real a historical justification, that they are held with a Covenanting austerity and passion, and that they have done much to keep manhood alive in those whom the conditions of life and work might well have degraded to the pit of animalism. The Church has to face a new religion, which it must humanise and transform or fail in its mission.

Side by side with this industrial congestion has gone the emptying of the countryside. The Highlands have long been depopulated, and have become in large part a parasitic society, dependent upon the money spent by alien sportsmen. More serious is the recent decay of many Lowland districts. The old, compact, rural society is disappearing.   Some of the best of our country stocks, under economic stress, have drifted into the cities to swell the confusion, or have carried their strength and skill overseas. All of us know glens where in our childhood half a dozen homesteads smoked, and where now the only inhabitants are a shepherd and his dog.

With these obvious changes has come a subtler one—a steady flattening out under the steam-roller of time of many familiar features in our Scottish landscape. Some of our ancient institutions would appear to be decaying, and there is a general loss of idiom and individuality in Scottish life. We can boast to-day of no school of Scottish philosophy, Scottish art or Scottish letters. The vernacular is little spoken or understood ; in the towns the speech is merely a broadened and dilapidated English ; Scots survives only as a book tongue. Even as such it runs a risk of being crushed out in the mill of a standardised education, and, should this happen, we shall have lost the power of truly appreciating that part of our literary heritage which is most triumphantly our own—the best of the Ballads, Burns and Sir Walter Scott. It is not surprising that, faced with such evidences of the loss of national birthrights, there should be Scotsmen who would revise the Act of Union even at the expense of political confusion and economic loss.

The difficulties are great, but I believe that they can be overcome ; the losses are already grievous, but they can be made good. Scotland has always had one gift above others, the power of adapting herself to altered circumstances, of accepting novelties and making them her own. She has joined these new things to her existing life, and moulded them to her national shape. She has been always deeply conscious of her past, believing that to break with it was to break with the future. Her supreme national talent has been her instinct for unification, her ability to be open-minded, adaptable and receptive, but, whenever she admitted

a change, to link it organically to her existing
life. That is her business to-day in the face
of far more startling novelties than any in
her history. She has to accept changes, but
to make sure that in the process of change
she does not sacrifice those qualities and
institutions which have built up her historic
character. She has to link a new world with
an old. I believe that there is vitality and
to spare for this purpose ; but a leader is
needed if she is to keep what she cherishes
in the older Scotland, and at the same time
adapt herself courageously to the demands
of the new. And her natural leader, now
as in the past, is that Church which is her
most idiomatic possession.

IV

PROSPICE

In economics this is the day of great
aggregations. The increasing complexity of
the conditions of life and the growth of

population have compelled mankind for the
sake of bare existence to band itself in larger
units. The movement, which has been conspicuous in national industry, is already
spreading beyond national frontiers. We
are tending towards big combinations both
for production and marketing—a rational
consequence of the drawing of the globe into
closer contacts. This world-wide impulse
has been reflected in the Christian Church.
There has been a steady progress towards
union among the non-episcopal Churches in
Britain and the Dominions, in the United
States, and on the Continent of Europe.
In India there has been a movement of the
first importance towards a unity of all
evangelical communions. And the sources
of this new impulse have been those which
have given us Church union in Scotland—
a simplifying of confessions, a distinguishing
of what is essential in Church polity from
what is accidental, and a recognition of the
need for a unified command and a united

battle-front in the face of a supreme necessity. Everywhere men are realising that
sentiment and tradition, however cherished,
must be sacrificed to an imperious duty, and
that if the Church is to carry its banners to
victory it must discard the irrelevant and
concentrate upon realities.

Is it not possible that a united Church of
Scotland may play a leading part in such a
hopeful crusade ? Its confessions are firmly
based upon the Evangel of Christ. It is
long-descended, with a famous ancestry.
Its polity is no casual, inorganic, atomic
thing, but an organism richly differentiated.
In the words of Rainy's great definition,
Presbyterianism means " organised life, regulated distribution of forces, graduated recognition of gifts, freedom to discuss, authority
to control, agency to administer." It is in
tune with what is best in democracy, for it is
" a system for a free people that love a
regulated, a self-regulating freedom." The
world to-day is being forced to relinquish

much of its traditional baggage, but at the same time it longs for proof of continuity. There are many hard problems yet to be solved before we are in sight even of Protestant union, many more before there is hope of a united Christendom ; but the impulse is there, and it is difficult to believe that it will weaken, since it is in accord with a universal impulse in secular life. May not a united Church of Scotland play in the future the part of a *brücke-Kirche* between Churches rich in historic accretions and Churches which lack them, since it has been resolute both to discard and to retain ?

Sed nondum est finis. As we watch the start on the road our mood must be one of mingled confidence and humility. In the mists of the future lie tremendous possibilities of both triumph and failure. The Church carries with it the destiny of coming generations of our countrymen, and of that beloved and ancient and mystical thing, our Scottish

fatherland. Its hope is less in its new structure than in the spirit which inspires it, a
keener and more vigilant purpose, a spirit of
brotherhood and charity, since the old
unhappy things have become far off and
forgotten. Matthew Arnold, in his poem
" Sohrab and Rustum," describes how the
Oxus flows through the " hushed Choras-
mian waste," and how the sands split its
currents and dam its streams, until at last
the dash of waves is heard, and the river
finds enlargement and peace in the great
sea. It has been so with our Church. It
began with the bright speed of a mountain
stream, but soon it found its course split and
divided, and too often in the last three
centuries it has been a " foiled circuitous
wanderer." Now once again its currents
are united, " brimming and bright and
large," and united it flows into the deserts
of a world which had never more need of its
reviving power. And somewhere in the far
distance it may find, like Oxus, a still

greater union—in that ocean to which the streams of every Christian Church will pour their waters—

                           wide
And tranquil, from whose floor the new-bathed
    stars
Emerge and shine upon the Aral sea.

INDEXED IN *subject*
need

R0159044912   HUM   285.
                        2411
                        B918

BUCHAN, JOHN
      KIRK IN SCOTLAND
1560 1929

R0159044912 ✓ HUM   285.
                        2411
                        B918

HOUSTON PUBLIC LIBRARY

CENTRAL LIBRARY
500 MCKINNEY

5